COMPETITION

AND

CHEATING

Books in the

**FUNDAMENTAL AWARENESS
IN ECONOMICS AND POLITICS**

series

Book One

LOSING SOCIAL INTELLECT

The core reason behind the troubles in
Free Market Economy and Democracy

Fundamental Awareness
in Economics and Politics

BOOK TWO

COMPETITION
AND
CHEATING

The malfunctioning of
Free Market Economy and Democracy

SALIH REISOGLU

Book Two published in 2025

ISBN 979-8-9922272-0-8

Contents

INTRODUCTION

The latest decades have witnessed the continuation and the further rise of the economic and political troubles in the western societies. Economic growth stays inadequate unless very loose fiscal policies are applied, while such policies are unsustainable as they further rise the already skyrocketing public debt and the accompanying inflation. Income and wealth inequalities are at unacceptable levels and do not show any signs of falling - if not rising further. Democracies are witnessing the emergence of populists or extremists, replacing the rational thinkers and the moderates. All in all, the welfare of the societies are declining.

Most western societies are stuck in such a miserable condition as a result of *the major structural problems that remain uncured in their economic and political systems*. One is the loss of the Social Intellect of the societies relative to the rising complexity of the world, as discussed in Book One of this series. And another is *the violation of the principles of competition and the further spreading of cheating, corruption, and concentration of power within their economic and political systems*, which will be the focus of this second book.

THE SCOPE OF THE DISCUSSION

In economics and politics, everything is dependent on almost everything else, but it is impossible to examine such a complex system of relations by considering all variables simultaneously. Therefore, first the main pieces of the puzzle will be examined one by one through the books in this series, and when all the pieces are complete by the end of the series, the full picture will emerge.

Competition and Cheating, the second book in the series, focuses on competition, cheating and concentrations of power, and the roles they play within the two pillars of the western social order, namely Free Market Economy and Democracy.

Within the framework of the series, Book Two builds on the concepts introduced in Book One, and together they pave the way for Book Three and Four of the series. Still, to keep Book Two as a stand alone reference, brief explanations or reviews of topics in Book One are given wherever necessary.

NO SPECIFIC SOCIETY IS TARGETED, BUT ALL ARE COVERED

As in all the books in this series, although no countries are mentioned, the primary focus of the discussion will seem to be on the economically advanced western societies. However, all the discussed issues, analyses and potential remedies mentioned in the books can be applied to any society that exercises a Free Market Economy and Democracy.

THE STYLE OF THE BOOK

The *Fundamental Awareness in Economics and Politics* series combine economics and politics, and therefore belong to a rather niche category. Although the discussions focus on the practical realities as much as the principles, the books in the series are still based on social sciences, and in that regard, many comments and concluding remarks have to be constructed to reflect the completeness and preciseness of scientific rationale. Still, the books are written in plain English rather than in a scientific jargon, so that any reader interested in economics and politics can easily follow the flow of the ideas.

Thanks to the free flow of information and the availability of a huge supply of it, and the new attention attracters growing exponentially within the digital media, most of us now have ultra short spans of attention. In line with this reality, I will not repeat the already-known and well-understood, but only concentrate on the significant but neglected or misunderstood. To respect the time and to keep the attention of the reader, I will make all arguments as sharp and as short as possible.

I kindly request the readers to integrate the pieces of the puzzle as they read through the books in this series, and to adopt the conclusions to their own societies.

Chapter 1

FREEDOM, EQUALITY AND FAIRNESS

1.1   A Glimpse of the Past

The Problem In Our Creation

Mankind is created with two ills. We are born *unequal*. And this is *unfair*.

Luck, a destroyer of fairness, starts to play its part, and probably its most significant one, at the very day one is born. Some are wise. Some are beautiful. Some are healthy and strong. Some are born into a rich or intellectual family. Some are born in a major city in an advanced society, at a time of prosperity and peace. Some are all. And some are none.

People being born unequal is actually a gift for the mankind, as it is the clashes of different behaviour of the individuals that enable the economic, political and social development of the societies. But what is a gift for mankind, and thus for the society, may be a curse for many individuals, as differences come both in the form of superiorities and inferiorities. And that is not fair.

Following its creation, mankind wished to cure both these ills, failing to realize the contradiction in between.

THE TIE-BREAKER

When mankind also desired *freedom*, he realized that *freedom and equality are mutually exclusive*, as freedom destroys equality -even if it had existed initially-, simply because individual choices (hard work, risk taking attitude, cheating) and randomness (luck) play their part in shaping a unique future for each individual.

While freedom and equality are mutually exclusive, freedom and fairness are not. *Freedom does not naturally introduce fairness, but it does not contradict with fairness either.*

Therefore, although fairness and equality sound similar on the surface, they are actually quite different: fairness can live with freedom, while equality can not. And *as the society can not sacrifice freedom, the natural choice is clear: equality can not and should not exist, while fairness can and should.*

A MATTER OF CHOICE

The relationship between freedom and equality is clear and rigid: freedom contradicts with equality, and thus necessitates and validates inequality. This simple relation brings a simple conclusion: *a free society has to live with inequality.*

But the relationship between freedom and fairness is different, as freedom does not necessitate the existence or non-existence of fairness. And this fact enables us to reach two more conclusions.

First, *a free society does not have to live with unfairness.*

Second and more important, *if fairness will ever exist, it will be because of the intellectual choice of the society, rather than as a necessity or a consequence of freedom.*

The Value Of Freedom

When people are born unequal, those who are born at a disadvantage with respect to the average of the society naturally try hard to improve their position, and to achieve that they need freedom.

As an interesting but critical part of human nature, those born at an advantage also try hard to further improve their position and pass ahead of those who are even better than themselves. To achieve that, they need freedom too.

Consequently, most people are not satisfied with their current position, whatever it is, but rather try hard to do better than others to improve their relative position. And there is always somebody better and thus somebody to be passed.

This makes freedom a shared value and a shared demand of almost everybody at all times, making it the undisputed winner of the priority ranking among human values.

The Critical Ranking : Fairness vs Inequality

Freedom, fairness, equality. By the nature of mankind, people care about all of these values.

They care about freedom and want it.

They care about fairness and -sincerely or insincerely- want it.

And they care about equality, and do not want it. Just on the contrary, what they want is *inequality, provided that they are on the winning side* of that inequality.

All these are rational desires. The trouble, however, is the priorities between these three, which vary from individual to individual.

Freedom is the number one priority for almost everybody. However, the second and third priorities differ.

For many people, the second priority is fairness. Inequality comes last. For these people, being on the winning side of inequality is desired if and only if it does not contradict with fairness. We will call such people *Fair Players*. They stick to ethics at any cost.

However, for many other people, the second priority is being on the winning side of inequality. Fairness, if it enters the rankings at all, is the last one, provided that it does not contradict with establishing inequality to their advantage. We will call such people *Cheaters*. For them, ethics is a city in another country for other people to live in – and preferably a much more crowded city than their own.

And whether the Fair Players or the Cheaters dominate the society is the primary determinant of the fate of the society.

Choices For The Social Order Of The Society

Historically societies have structured their social orders based on their primary preference regarding the three fundamental values of mankind. As freedom and equality can not co-exist, and fairness can not exist without freedom, in principle societies have only the following four choices:

- *Pure-Equality* : Equality, without freedom and without fairness.
- *Pure-Freedom* : Freedom, without equality and without fairness.
- *Freedom-and-Fairness* : Fairness within freedom, without equality.
- *None-of-the-Three* : None of equality, freedom or fairness.

The last choice is the worst, as the society sacrifices all three values simultaneously. Unfortunately, mankind's social adventure started from there, at the times of monarchies and minority reigns. Naturally, with the first tiny flicker of intellect, mankind started to struggle to get out of that miserable situation. The rest of the story has already been told by the historians, so I will skip that and move to the recent times, to the competition between the other three choices.

As will be discussed in detail in the coming chapters, defenders of *Freedom-and-Fairness*, including the Author of this series, argue that *inequality is a price to be paid for fairness, provided that inequality arises based on Fair Competition and remains within acceptable levels*. The argument continues that *the society must value, promote and guard fairness, not only because it is ethical, but primarily because it maximises both the individuals' and the society's material and social interests and overall welfare in the long run*.

Defenders of *Pure-Equality* argue that, perfect fairness is impossible to achieve, since, even if equal opportunity is provided by the society at the beginning, people are not born equal and thus there is an unfairness at birth that can not be cured ever after. Plus, luck plays a significant part. Therefore, as perfect fairness can not be achieved, the society has to sacrifice both fairness and freedom, and stick to equality.

And there is no explicit defender of *Pure-Freedom*, as it is rather difficult to explain why fairness should be excluded once there is freedom, and thus why some people should be given the freedom to cheat.

Therefore, from a rational viewpoint, one may expect that defenders of *Pure-Equality* will compete with and lose against defenders of *Freedom-and-Fairness*, both for the desire for freedom and the preference for fairness within freedom. However, contrary to the rational expectation, in recent decades' practice, most societies, if not all, managed to end up at some social order close to *Pure-Freedom*.

A TOUCH OF RECENT HISTORY

This strange outcome is a result of the political environment of the recent decades, during which some concentrated interest groups benefiting from *Pure-Freedom* -as it enables them to cheat-, have exhibited a stellar performance on perception management, where they have presented only two options to the society, namely *Pure-Equality* and *Pure-Freedom*, and have successfully hidden the option of *Freedom-and-Fairness*. They have simply renamed the options as "equality" versus "freedom" within which the possibility of attaining fairness has been conveniently forgotten. Once the options were presented that way, the rest followed naturally. As all societies have sooner or later realized that equality is not the right option, a fact solidified further by the fall of the Soviet Republic, they were easily driven towards *Pure-Freedom*, completely missing the best option, namely *Freedom-and-Fairness*. And once fallen in, escaping from this trap is not easy, unless a society develops an adequate level of Social Intellect.

Adequate Social Intellect, however, is still a practically distant condition even for the economically-advanced societies of the west, as demonstrated by the fact that even after the experience of the 2008 crisis, these societies still lack the necessary social awareness required to implement the required fundamental structural changes to cure their failing social orders.

As promised at the Introduction, without diving further into the well-known developments of the recent past, we will now go back to the basics.

Freedom Brings Competition

Freedom, as an inevitable consequence, brings competition. And competition is the main driver of innovation, economic growth and social development. However, just like freedom, competition neither contradicts nor demands fairness. Consequently, competition may or may not be fair. But in any case, competition introduces inequality.

Then, the main question regarding the appropriate structure of competition naturally comes out to be "How to decide who will be on the winning side of the inequality?". The answer will help to define the rules of competition.

In intellectually weak societies, these rules are conveniently set around the principle of free competition, leaving fairness out. However, free competition without fairness, breeds not only Fair Players, but also Cheaters who promote and protect their own interests at the expense of the rest of the society. Consequently, free competition without fairness brings *Excessive Inequality,* which in turn decreases the welfare of the society and threatens the stability of its social order in the long run.

In an intellectually advanced society, however, the concept of fairness should be integrated to the rules. Not solely free competition, but *Fair Competition* should decide who deserves to be on the winning side of the inequality.

Fair Competition will be discussed in detail in the next chapter. However, before that, its ever-rising importance needs to be clarified further, through taking a brief look at where the current trends will take the societies in the future.

1.2   A Glimpse of the Future

The Dangerous Relation Of Freedom And Inequality

Freedom and competition inevitably bring inequality. The society must therefore embrace inequality, but prevent it from rising to excessive levels, through establishing Fair Competition - or, as will be discussed in Book Three, in cases where that is not adequate, through taxation and redistribution.

As will be discussed in the coming chapters, if the society fails to establish Fair Competition, cheating will spread, and consequently, concentrated economic powers may emerge. These concentrated economic powers will then seek political influence to protect themselves from both competition and taxation, and to serve that purpose, they may support the emergence of some concentrated political power with which they can cooperate. The concentrated economic and political powers will then promote their own interests against those of the society. Consequently, Free Market Economy and Democracy will cease to serve the society's interests, and inequality will reach excessive levels, decreasing the welfare of the society.

Therefore, although freedom is the main pillar of the western social order based on Free Market Economy and Democracy, if it is not accompanied by the Social Intellect of the society, it will pave the way for the self-destruction of the western social order.

Apocalypse On The Horizon

The trouble with the relation of freedom and inequality, namely the ever-rising greed and the resulting tendency to cheat, will itself exponentially worsen in the coming decades for two related reasons already on the horizon.

MAGNIFYING INEQUALITY AT BIRTH

In each individual's story of life, luck starts to play its part at birth, as some people are lucky to be born intelligent and beautiful, into a rich family, in an advanced society, etc., while others may have no such chance. Unfair as it may be, it at least *seems* to be the outcome of a natural lottery.

The reality, unfortunately, does not coincide with what it seems. In many cases, people who are intelligent and/or rich, mate with others within their own society who are like themselves. Thus, their children have a much higher genetic probability to be intelligent and are already born into rich families in advanced societies. Based on their intelligence, and backed by their family wealth, they most probably get educated at the best universities, where they again meet their mates with similar qualifications. And the story repeats generation after generation, amplifying the advantage at birth each time. Needless to say, the opposite works just in the same way, where poverty or any mental weakness also amplifies itself with each generation. Thus, what is initially considered as luck at birth, is not a random luck, but rather a result of genetics combined with statistics for very many cases, magnifying the inequality at birth more and more with each generation.

As if this is not enough, in the coming decades, the scientific developments regarding biology and genetics, will enable those parents who can afford it, to manipulate and improve both the physical and the mental characteristics of their children before they are born, to create a definite superiority at birth, further amplifying the inequality at birth within the society.

To make matters even worse, for those who can afford it, including the ones already born into golden cradles with already superior mental and physical abilities, the upgrading of human body and mind will soon continue all through their lifetimes, continuously amplifying the inequality to their benefit.

A couple of generations later, the society will end up with a small group of winners who are superior and are well aware that they are superior, and crowds of losers who also know that they are inferior. To have a glimpse of how things will proceed in such a society, just consider two simple facts. On the one hand, even if a social security net is established, it may not be sustainable, as the winners may not be willing to support the losers forever. And on the other hand, the losers may look for some fundamental changes in the social order, as being kept alive only by the generosity of the winners (some of whom will not even be fair winners) may not feel great for their self-esteem and dignity. This will not be a society anybody would like to live in, including the winners.

To dramatically finalize the doomsday scenario, consider the competition among the winners. Even if they belong to a small Homo-Superior race within a crowd of Homo-Sapiens, they will still struggle for further inequality among themselves, as the desire to be comparatively better than those in their vicinity will still exist as a consequence of the never-diminishing animal spirits in humans. So, next, the Homo-Superior will try to become Superior-Squared, and then Superior-Cubed, in a struggle that will go on forever – continuously decreasing the ratio of winners and increasing the ratio of losers within the society, and shouting farewell to social peace.

LOSING EQUALITY AT DEATH

Although people are born unequal and that is unfair, at least they all die equal and that is sort of fair. Moreover, as their lifetimes are limited and it is impossible to carry their assets to the other side with them, they are assumed to have a diminishing return on accruing wealth, which supposedly decreases their greed and aggressiveness against others.

Fortunately for some, and unfortunately for the society, the recent developments in biological engineering and related fields are bringing mankind to the point where more wealth may eventually buy people more time, more life. Although death may still be unescapable for some more time, a significant increase in lifespans for those who can pay for it is becoming a reality. Thus, the assumed diminishing return on accruing wealth -and the accompanying weakening of greed- may soon become a phenomenon of the past.

It does not require a genius to guess the potential effect of these developments on human greed and aggressiveness, or, on the tendency to cheat in the competition, whose prize for winners is now further lifetime, and punishment for losers is (otherwise avoidable) untimely death.

What all this means is that, on the one hand, the competition for wealth will get ever fiercer and the urge to cheat to maximise one's personal benefits will become ever more irresistible in the not-so-distant future, increasing the aggressiveness of all competitors. On the other hand, the loss of equality even at death will increase the aggressiveness of the losers against the existing social order and the winners. This, clearly, is an unfortunate combination, and will not help to sustain social peace.

TIME IS NOT ON OUR SIDE

These potential developments on the horizon and the danger they create for the stability of the social order of the society makes the proper handling of Fair Competition and inequality urgent issues with utmost significance.

In light of a glimpse of the past and a glimpse of the future, the society has to realize what it needs to do today and act in time.

Unfortunately, the awareness of the society on these issues is only marginal, thanks to its lagging intellectual level compared to the extreme speeds and magnitudes of technological, economical and social developments of the latest decades. Therefore, as already discussed in detail in Book One, now may be the last chance to channel all the necessary resources to boost the Social Intellect of the society, as there is no other precaution that may stand against the doomsday scenario mentioned above.

Chapter 2

FAIR COMPETITION

2.1   Allocation Of Resources & Social Intellect

Allocation Of Resources

In both economics and politics, demand and supply meet to form the equilibrium desired by the society. In economics the subject is the availability and pricing of goods and services, in politics it is the rule making (legislation) and the governance (execution). Within this macro picture, each individual plays his micro role. On the demand side, each individual acts as a consumer and a voter. On the supply side, in economics he acts as some sort of supplier of physical or mental labour, and in politics he may act as a Politician.

The macro-equilibrium in both economics and politics forms through a chain of interactions between the individual and the society. *Each individual has personal demand preferences as a consumer and a voter, that are primarily shaped by his Social Intellect.* Individual demands add up to create the society's macro-demand. In turn, the macro-supply of the society forms in reaction to that macro-demand, and each individual adjusts his personal micro-supply to fit into somewhere within that macro-supply. And through this chain reaction the overall equilibrium, and thus the resource allocation within the society, emerges.

To appreciate the scope and the importance of this observation, it will help to clarify what is meant by resources. One easy to guess component of the society's resources is the physical ones. These not only include the natural resources, but also cover labour, thus the physical capacity of a society's human resources. Another easy to guess component is financial resources. But more important are the scientific and technical resources, including the accumulated know-how within the society. And the most important is the mental capacity of the human resources of the society. The society's welfare will change one way or another depending on where and how these limited resources are allocated. The more intellectual the society gets, the better will be this allocation and consequently the higher will be the society's welfare[1].

The concept of allocation of resources covers a much wider and much more significant spectrum than commonly realised. For instance, the society needs to decide whether scientific research or entertainment should have a higher priority in allocating its financial resources. Or, whether the best mental resources of the society, namely their brightest minds, should be primarily allocated to private financial sector or to politics and the state. There are very many dimensions among which the resources of the society have to be distributed, and the appropriate allocation will change over time and under different conditions.

However, there are two critical issues regarding resource allocation, that remain to be valid under all conditions and at all times.

First, the society's preferences and decisions that shape the resource allocation should be formed and made rationally in order to maximise the welfare of the society in the long run. And at the heart of rationality lies the *Social Intellect of the society*, which was the main theme of the first book in this series and will be briefly reviewed next.

Second, the demand and supply should meet under appropriate competitive conditions for the formation of the optimal resource allocation. And at the heart of the appropriate competitive conditions lies *Fair Competition*, which is one of the main themes of this book and will be discussed in the following section.

Social Intellect

From an economic and political perspective, what counts as intellect is *Social Intellect*, which *is a balanced blend of intelligence, social education, social experience and social awareness.*

Having adequate Social Intellect, therefore, can be defined as having some basic education and accumulated experience in *social sciences* that improve an individual's *awareness of the social environment* around him, both as a political participant (at least as a voter) and as an economic participant (at least as a consumer and a supplier of labour) in the society.

And social education must span the basics of the primary social sciences of politics, economics, finance, law and sociology. In common practise, societies and individuals try their best to invest in education targeting professional expertise in many specific fields, and produce many experts who add value to the society and increase its welfare, but unfortunately, *such professional education is not social education, and does not enable an individual to have adequate Social Intellect.*

Needless to say, the aim of social education is not, and can not be, to create an economics or politics expert out of each individual. All that is required of social education is to make each member of the society intellectual enough to be able to understand and evaluate the analysis of the real experts in social sciences, so that he can attain and keep social awareness, and make rational decisions as a consumer and a voter.

Finally, social awareness is the continuous process of spending time and effort to observe and understand the developments in economics and politics within and out of the society. Therefore, access to complete and correct information on the developments and to the analyses of the experts are also required. As will be discussed in the coming chapters, although the societies may still not realise the significance of attaining and sustaining Social Intellect, the Cheaters in both economics and politics have long ago realised the need to prevent such social awareness.

SOCIAL INTELLECT IS A RELATIVE CONCEPT

It can be guessed from the explanation above that *Social Intellect is a relative concept*, as it concerns *the intellectual level of the society compared to the complexity of the economic and political environment in which it needs to survive.*

Therefore, *if the complexity in the economic and political environment is rising faster than the increase in the intellectual level of the society, then the Social Intellect of the society is actually falling in relative terms.* In other words, the more complex the world becomes, the relatively less intellectual the society gets, although in absolute terms its current members may actually be much better educated than those in the past generations. And when the relative Social Intellect of the society falls, the economic and political systems which are based on the assumption that the society remains intelligent enough, will not be working properly anymore.

Therefore, societies that used to be intellectually advanced in the past will become intellectually inadequate unless they can increase their average intellectual level and social awareness in pace with the increasing complexity of the world. And the complexity of the world is increasing at a never-before-seen pace, almost exponentially. And that is why even the economically advanced societies started to fall behind and started to experience severe troubles in the latest decades in both their economic and political systems[2].

Social Intellect Is A Prerequisite For The Optimal Allocation Of Resources

The western social order, based on Free Market Economy and Democracy, assumes that individuals will act rationally, and by doing so, they will enable the optimal allocation of the society's resources such that the society's welfare will be maximised. And acting rationally requires understanding *causations*, namely *the chain of events from the reason(s) to the result(s)*. And as the world becomes more and more complex, understanding causations is becoming more and more of a challenge for each individual.

In a world where there are mutual interactions among societies coupled with many other emerging complications (like technological developments or ageing of societies), the causation-relations are getting exponentially complex. To start with, now there are too many reasons (variables -in scientific jargon) effecting any result (outcome -in scientific jargon). And worse, in the way expressed in scientific jargon, the relation of the outcome to the variables is non-linear. In simple terms, this means that how a certain change in a certain variable effects the outcome also depends on the simultaneous changes on other variables[3], making the understanding of the overall relation and thus forecasting the potential outcome of any action extremely difficult.

These create a terribly difficult world for the societies to understand. On the one hand, as the world is changing fast and a lot, and that is effecting every society, *the optimal allocation of resources for each society must be changing over time*. On the other hand, the complex nature of the new world makes it *extremely difficult to understand how the optimal allocation must change*.

Therefore, in order to be able to make rational decisions on all sorts of complex issues, societies first need to rise their Social Intellect to adequate levels. This makes *Social Intellect a prerequisite for the optimal allocation of resources* within a society.

And Social Intellect Is A Prerequisite For More

Social Intellect is necessary but unfortunately not enough to attain optimal resource allocation. As we have briefly mentioned above, and will discuss in detail in the next section, to have optimal allocation of resources, demand and supply should reach their equilibrium within a market environment of Fair Competition. However, *Social Intellect is a prerequisite for Fair Competition* as well, since the higher the Social Intellect of a society, the closer the society can get to Fair Competition.

Finally, as we will see in the later chapters, *Social Intellect is also a prerequisite for preventing the spread of cheating and corruption* within the economic and political systems.

2.2   Fair Competition

The Passion For Fairness

Richard Thaler, the father of behavioural economics, presents a simple game on fairness in his book Misbehaving[4], based on which he had run many experiments. In this game there are two players between whom a fixed amount of money will be shared. The first player has the right to offer which proportion each will get, and the second player has the right to accept or reject that offer. If he rejects, neither player will receive anything. The rational expectations approach, taught in business schools, runs the logic that, as long as the second player has any share in the distribution offered by the first, he should accept the offer, since any amount larger than zero will mean a net benefit for the second player. And knowing this, the first player will only offer a minimal share to the second and get away with most of the money. However, the experiments revealed that life does not work that way in practise. If the second player feels that the distribution of shares is too unfair, he almost always chooses to reject the offer, making both of them worse off. Thus, people are ready to pay a price in order to reject unfairness.

In these experiments, rejecting unfairness is solely based on the behavioural characteristics of humans. When they think rationally, however, they have even stronger incentives to demand fairness, as will become clear by the end of this section.

Free Competition : Necessary But Not Enough

Economics theory states that, in a free (and therefore competitive) market, supply and demand meet and balance out each other, to reveal the so-called equilibrium market price for a good or service. Guided by this price mechanism, the market participants on both the supply and the demand sides can determine how they should allocate their resources in the most appropriate manner. The maximisation of the welfare of the society requires this optimal allocation of resources, and that in turn requires adherence to the principles of competition by all participants.

In the classic economic literature, the best way to create optimal conditions is believed to be creating free and perfect competition, in the sense that there must be no barriers to entry and exit, and no single competitor should be able to effect the price formation in the market. These are necessary, but unfortunately, not enough to bring optimal allocation of resources. To achieve optimal allocation, we need *Fair Competition,* which is a concept beyond the classic definition of free and perfect competition.

However, before proceeding to discuss what Fair Competition is, it is important to clarify that, although the discussion of competition usually focuses on the supply side alone, actually *both sides of the market have to be subject to Fair Competition to reach the optimal outcome.* This is simply because, while the competition between producers tend to decrease the price, the competition between consumers tend to increase the price, and that is how the market clearing price, where total production equals total consumption, should emerge. For that reason, only when Fair Competition exists on both sides, the optimal price will be formed to enable the optimal allocation of resources and to maximise the welfare of the society in the long run.

Fair Competition : The Three Conditions

Fair Competition requires the fulfilment of all the three conditions below on both the supply and the demand sides. Therefore, it extends beyond free and perfect competition (which is by itself the second condition below) and necessitates the fulfilment of the first and third conditions as well.

(1) *Fair opportunity for all competitors in getting prepared for the competition.*

(2) *Free and perfect competition, where all competitors compete under exactly the same rules (and none can effect the making of the rules or can be permitted to violate the rules), there are no barriers to entry or exit, and no single competitor can effect the price formation in the market.*

(3) The existence of proper regulation to ensure that the rules of competition are set and enforced to protect and promote the long-term interests of the society, beyond balancing the interests of those who participate in the market as producers on the supply side and as consumers on the demand side.

Next, we will discuss what these conditions mean for each side from an economic perspective. However, all these conditions are valid for establishing Fair Competition in politics as well, as will be discussed partially in the later chapters and in more detail in Book Four of this series.

The First Condition

FAIR OPPORTUNITY ON THE SUPPLY SIDE

Fair opportunity on the supply side is required to make sure that *all the right candidates should be able to join the competition*, where the term right candidate refers to *those with the highest potential to succeed in competition and thus create the highest value for both the demand side and the society*. Otherwise, a competition among incapables will not result in an optimal distribution of resources and thus will fail to maximise the welfare of the society. It is amazing to see that, although fair opportunity is the starting point of Fair Competition in the market, societies are far away from understanding the significance of it, let alone achieving it, as an unfortunate result of the inadequacy of their Social Intellect.

FAIR OPPORTUNITY FOR HUMAN RESOURCES

On the supply side, candidates for competition are mostly considered to be the corporations, however, within a corporate structure it is the human capital that makes most of the difference. Furthermore, under today's conditions, it is probably the only source of difference, as capital has a diminishing importance in an environment where it became abundant. Therefore, it is vital for every society to make sure that it gives a fair opportunity to all its members and let the most capable ones proceed further.

Fair opportunity for human resources means that the more capable an individual, the more opportunity he has to be given at both education and employment, without any practical limitations. Otherwise, optimal allocation of resources will not be possible.

Notice that *fair opportunity is not the same as equal opportunity.* Equal opportunity in practise is mostly an equality at the bare minimums. But fair opportunity has to go beyond that. If opportunities for education and employment are minimal, this is equal but not fair.

For instance, if all children are given an opportunity to study up to the end of the middle school, this is equal, but not fair. Those with higher abilities must be given the opportunity to continue all the way up – till the end of a post graduate degree if they want. Similarly, if young adults can only find relatively unqualified jobs, this is equal but not fair. Those with higher capabilities (and thus higher education) must be given the opportunity to find more qualified jobs, and rise all the way up later on in their career.

For *fair opportunity* to reach beyond equal opportunity, *each individual should have adequate access both to the education he deserves and to the employment he deserves, solely based on his personal capabilities.*

If there is a certain barrier level in education and employment beyond which only the selected few can reach (where the selection is not based on individual capabilities, but mostly on the financial power or the social network of one's family, or worse, based on gender, race, religion or some other sort of social-belonging to some privileged group), then having equal opportunity only at the bottom does not mean anything.

Unfortunately, in almost all societies, having equal opportunity at the bare minimums is considered to be enough to satisfy the conditions of some sort of competition that is somehow expected to maximise the wealth and the welfare of the society. Or, from another viewpoint, as will be discussed in the coming chapters, the Cheaters have been doing a good job in diverting the attention of the society away from such fundamental conditions required for rising the welfare of the society, conveniently benefiting themselves at the expense of the society.

COMPARATIVE ADVANTAGE AND OPTIMAL ALLOCATION OF
HUMAN RESOURCES

To better understand why fair opportunity for both education and
employment is a necessity, it will help to clarify the concept of
Comparative Advantage[5].

In simple terms, optimal allocation of resources requires adherence to
the principle of *Comparative Advantage* which states that *each individual
should do what he can do best relative to the others*.

This sounds so simple in principle, but in practise life gets complicated.
First, *what* an individual can do best and *how good* he can do it depends
very much on his education. Second, allocation of resources in line with
this principle requires adequate job mobility that is not constrained by
shadow barriers.

As a simple illustration of the concept, consider a tiny society. This
society needs two products, X and Y, that can be produced by either of
two people, A and B.

In the initial case, there is no fair opportunity, and A is well educated while
B is not. And thus, their production capabilities are:

Educated-A can produce either product X (say 20 units of X each worth
$0.5) with a total value of $10 to the society, or product Y (say 5 units of
Y each worth $1) with a total value of $5 to the society, within a certain
time period.

Uneducated-B can produce either product X (say 6 units of X each worth
$0.5) with a total value of $3 to the society, or product Y (say 4 units of Y
each worth $1) with a total value of $4 to the society, within the same
time period.

In this initial case, Educated-A can produce more of both products within
the time period, and thus he has absolute advantage over Uneducated-
B in both. However, each person can specialise in only one product in
practise, thus they need to allocate jobs of producing X and Y among
themselves. Then, there are two possibilities:

Educated-A can produce X with a total value of $10 and Uneducated-B can produce Y with a total value of $4, resulting in a total value of $14 for the society.

Alternatively, Educated-A can produce Y with a total value of $5 and Uneducated-B can produce X with a total value of $3, resulting in a total value of $8 for the society.

Within these two possibilities, the benefit of the society is maximised when Educated-A produces X and Uneducated-B produces Y, as the total value of their combined production for the society is higher ($14).

In the economics jargon, Educated-A is said to have a comparative advantage in producing X rather than Y, over Uneducated-B. This is because, although A can produce both products better than B, his capability to produce X with respect to B is much superior than his capability to produce Y with respect to B.

Next, consider the case where B is given a fair opportunity for both education and employment. Then the production capabilities of Educated-B change and a new situation emerges:

Educated-A can still produce either product X with a total value of $10 to the society, or product Y with a total value of $5 to the society, within a certain time period.

But Educated-B can now produce either product X with a total value of $20 to the society, or product Y with a total value of $6 to the society, within the same time period.

And now, the possibilities in job allocation become:

Educated-A can produce X with a total value of $10 and Educated-B can produce Y with a total value of $6, resulting in a total value of $16 for the society.

Alternatively, Educated-A can produce Y with a total value of $5 and Educated-B can produce X with a total value of $20, resulting in a total value of $25 for the society.

Within these two possibilities, the benefit of the society is maximised when Educated-A produces Y and Educated-B produces X, as the total value of their combined production for the society is higher ($25).

This very simple illustration has significant conclusions.

First, *having only a fair opportunity for education is not enough for the optimal allocation of resources, but a fair opportunity for employment is also required.* In the simple illustration above, if B is only educated but not allowed to switch jobs with A, then the total value of their combined production, where A still produces X and B still produces Y, will only rise to $16. However, when there is also a fair opportunity for employment, thus B is allowed to take the job of A, then the total value of their combined production will be maximised at $25.

The significance of the difference between having a fair opportunity for employment or not, can be better understood if we assume that the cost of educating B is $3 for the society. Then, without the fair opportunity for employment, the society will actually be worse off by educating B, as the immense rise in B's improved capability in producing X will be wasted. In the illustration above, if B can not switch jobs, the society will actually end up at ($16 - $3 =) $13, which is worse than the initial case where the society had $14. However, when B can switch jobs, the society will end up at ($25 - $3 =) $22, which is way above the initial case of $14.

Second, *if A is a Cheater, he will do all he can to either prevent a fair opportunity for education and/or a fair opportunity for employment for B, so that B can not overtake his job.* Notice that, assuming each individual gets a certain ratio of his production value as his personal income, A prefers to continue to produce X and thus get compensated more, although the consequence of such an allocation of jobs is terrible for the society - as the society ends up receiving $14 instead of $25 (or, $22 if education of B is costly) when A keeps his job.

Unfortunately, variations of such hidden cheating is common in most societies. In relatively more intellectual societies where having no opportunity even for education will sound too bad and attract too much criticism, the fair opportunity for education is given upto some extent to save the outlook, but the fair opportunity for employment is conveniently forgotten.

An intellectually advanced society, therefore, has to make sure that there are no shadow barriers based on race, beliefs or gender, that practically reserve certain professions or jobs to certain groups or minorities. To reach optimal resource allocation, which in turn will help to maximise the welfare of the society, the existence of *fair opportunity for both education and employment* must be demanded by the society.

ACHIEVING FAIR OPPORTUNITY IN EDUCATION

Fair opportunity starts with professional education. As a first step to optimise its allocation of human resources, *a society should make sure that the individuals with the highest merit have access to the best of education available, without facing financial obstacles.*

Some of those merited individuals may be able to afford a good education themselves, but those who can not must definitely be financed by the society. One classic way of doing this is extending bank credits backed by the state to the merited individuals, such that they will pay it back in their later years, and thus their education will not be a burden on the society. But a much better way would be creating a system of education insurance (free of charge) by the state, covering all the young individuals who deserve to be well educated but do not have access to adequate financial resources, all through their education provided that they continue to have a successful track record as they proceed to higher levels of education. Actually, such insurance should also cover their financing needs for proper nutrition and healthcare, as long as they continue to climb up the ladder of education. At first glance, such an insurance scheme may seem like an additional burden on the society, as these merited individuals will not be made to pay back anything later on. However, such a scheme is actually a great *social investment* that the society makes for its own future, as a better allocation of human resources will significantly improve the value created for the society in the long run, as explained above. Moreover, this scheme will not create a terribly demotivating financial burden on these merited individuals during the initial years of their employment, and thus will improve their professional performance further.

It is crucial to reemphasize that, the continuation of financing through the education insurance described above should be based on the successful performance of each individual demonstrated at every step of his continuing education. The fair opportunity in education structured this way is a great allocation of the financial resources of the society, as it is an investment that will create additional value for the society in the long run. However, an unconditional over-opportunity, namely spending too much on those who have limited capability, will be a misallocation of the financial resources of the society and a terrible investment, and should be avoided.

Finally, in cases where the society has a limited capacity of high quality professional education, especially at the university level, it should make sure that it is not wasting that capacity: when the resources are scarce, if the wrong person gets what he does not deserve (for some wrong reason like being born into a rich family), the right person loses his fair chance, and thus the total value to be created for the society in the long run significantly diminishes.

ACHIEVING FAIR OPPORTUNITY IN EMPLOYMENT

Fair opportunity for employment is necessary for the optimal allocation of human resources of a society. Otherwise, the educated human capital will either be wasted in relatively-less-qualified professional occupations, or move to join another society where their professional education will create more value. The second phenomenon is well recognized, as issues of immigration and brain-drain are discussed frequently in literature. However, the first phenomenon, namely wasting a society's own human capital within its own unfair job market, stays well hidden, especially in advanced economies where being semi-wasted within one's own society remains to be a preferable choice relative to the hassle of moving to another society and risking to succeed there. The harm that the society endures as a result of such mismanagement of the allocation of human resources comes rather slowly, and thus goes unnoticed, but it accumulates to a significant loss on the economic growth of the society in the long run.

As will be discussed in the later chapters, if a corporation has concentrated economic power or a monopoly position in a market, it faces much less competition and thus has the luxury of selecting its human resources based on preferences like race, beliefs, political view, gender or even kinship. Therefore, the only way to make sure that more capable individuals reach higher qualified professional positions and optimize the human resource allocation within the society, is to ensure that all markets function under competitive conditions at all times. Under that condition, each corporation has to look for the most capable candidates with the highest professional qualifications, in order to stay competitive and survive in its market.

FAIR OPPORTUNITY FOR CORPORATIONS

In most cases, it is not the human resources, but the corporations that take part in direct competition in the market. Therefore, for the best interest of the society, further measures have to be taken to enable young corporations with potential capabilities, to be given a fair opportunity in getting prepared for competition. This practically means they need to have at least enough opportunity in access to financing at rational prices (without paying excessive margins unproportional to their business risks), in accumulating know-how (without facing excessively long and protective intellectual property laws) and gathering human capital (without facing unfair binding or non-compete clauses that prevent the free movement of human resources), to name a few.

FAIR OPPORTUNITY ON THE DEMAND SIDE

Finally, fair opportunity on the demand side is required to make sure that all the potential consumers, namely anybody for whom the product has some value, have to be able to reach the market. Otherwise, a limited competition on the demand side will not bring out an optimal price, and thus the mispricing will cause a sub-optimal allocation of resources in the economy.

In practise, for most products, this means that any potential customer should have the purchasing power to join the market, so that the ones who value the product most can demand it. Achieving this, however, necessitates the availability of some basic income for all potential customers, and starts with the prevention of Excessive Inequality that causes many consumers to lose their purchasing power. The significant relation between inequality and demand, which is intuitively understandable up to some extent, will be discussed in detail in Book Three of this series.

The Second Condition

FREE AND PERFECT COMPETITION ON THE SUPPLY SIDE

The sub-conditions for free and perfect competition on the supply side are well known.

For free competition, there must be no barriers to entry and exit. In theory, when there are no barriers to entry or exit, any potential competitor willing to participate in the market should be able to join the competition, and any existing competitor willing to leave the market should be able to do so. In practise, however, there will always be some barriers based on either the nature of the market or the regulations governing that market. As long as such barriers are kept at a rational level, meaning that they are not unnecessarily strong or prohibitive, they will not prevent a healthy competition. Reading backwards, anyone (individual or corporation) willing to decrease competition for his own benefit and at the expense of all the other competitors and the society, will try to rise barriers for the others once he is in the market, as will be discussed in the coming chapters.

For perfect competition, no single producer or group of producers should be able to determine or even effect the price formation in the market, practically meaning that there must be no concentration of economic power in the market. Therefore, let alone the extreme cases of monopolies or oligopolies, any over-concentration that effects the price formation in a market will harm the optimal allocation of resources. For this reason, variations of anti-trust regulations are developed in almost all advanced economies.

Finally, all competitors should always be competing under exactly the same rules and regulations, meaning that no competitor should be able to violate or even bend the prevailing rules at any time, or effect the making of the rules by any means.

Although these are the classic and well-known principles regarding competition, most societies still fail to demand the adherence to even these rules and pay the price as sub-optimal growth and welfare. It is amazing to see that, during the latest decades societies are practically drafting away from even free and perfect competition, namely this second condition, let alone embracing the first and third conditions that will enable them to approach Fair Competition.

When free markets are left to their own devices, they tend to promote concentrations of economic power which in turn weaken or even destroy perfect competition. Therefore, regulatory intervention is required to ensure the continuation of perfect competition in the market. In practise, such intervention is supposed to be exercised under competition laws, also known as anti-trust laws, which involve the prevention of the formation or the breaking up of monopolies or any kind of over-concentration in the market. Unfortunately, the practical enforcement of competition laws has been very weak in the recent decades for many reasons, all of which can eventually be tied to a lack of political demand by the societies. Such demand, in turn, is dependent on the Social Intellect of the society.

Competition is also heavily wounded by the information asymmetry that naturally exists between the producers and consumers of a product or service. Such asymmetry is enough to distort the decisions of both sides, mostly to the benefit of the producers at the expense of the consumers, causing a diversion from the optimal pricing of the product in the market, and consequently a diversion from the optimal allocation of resources within the economy. Clearly, there is a need for regulatory intervention there as well, but unsurprisingly it is mostly missing.

FREE AND PERFECT COMPETITION ON THE DEMAND SIDE

Conditions similar to those for free and perfect competition on the supply side, are valid for the demand side.

For free competition, there must be no barriers to entry and exit, meaning that no consumer is prevented from joining the market and none is forced to consume either.

For perfect competition, no single consumer or a group of consumers should be able to determine or even effect the price formation in the market, practically meaning that there must be no monopoly or oligopoly of consumers either. This simple requirement became a major problem in the latest decades as many consumers are actually corporations themselves, and thus, those who hold monopoly positions in their own production markets on the supply side will probably hold monopoly positions in the markets in which they participate as consumers on the demand side. Therefore, the prevention of monopoly formations in any market, does not only serve the best interest of the consumers of that market, but also serves the interests of many suppliers in the other markets.

Finally, each corporation is a consumer on the demand side of the labour market of its own business, and thus, a monopoly formation will mean a loss of value for those individuals who happen to be on the supply side of that labour market, at least in the form of having to accept lower payments and weaker labour rights.

These multi dimensional negative effects reveal that the cost of monopolies to the society are much higher than actually realized by the society, but unfortunately the struggle against concentrations of economic power and monopolisation has continuously weakened during the latest decades.

The Third Condition

The third condition for Fair Competition states the necessity of proper regulation to ensure that the rules of competition in the market are set and enforced to protect and promote the long-term interests of the society. What this means in practise is that the outcome of the competition in the market should at least not harm the society, preferably create value for the society, and at best maximise the value created for the society.

Therefore, the society, through its political agents, namely the Legislative and Executive Bodies within the political system, must set the rules and enact regulations such that the society not only wins as a result of the competition defined by those rules and regulations, but also maximises its benefit from that competition by making it a fair one.

Naturally the third condition is the most vulnerable one for cheating purposes, simply because the society becomes defenceless once its Social Intellect weakens and consequently its political demand to protect its own interest disappears, while cheating is the easiest and the most beneficial when the society is the victim – as will be discussed in the coming chapters.

EXTERNALITIES

Even when the producers and consumers meet under conditions of free and perfect competition, and are both happy with the formation of the market price, the outcome may still not be beneficial for the society at large. This happens when the transaction they agree to execute may have consequences that effect some third parties within the society who are not on either side of the transaction. This creates a problem when these third parties are effected in a negative manner, practically meaning that they are unwillingly incurring a cost because of that transaction, called an *externality* in the jargon, which actually should have been paid by one or both of the sides taking part in the transaction.

One very well known and fashionable example of externalities is global warming, in which as a result of the production techniques utilized by the producers of certain goods, which some consumers are happily consuming, the whole global society is suffering. Unfortunately, many other externalities generated by various economic activities are not that well recognized, and thus the society pays a price without being aware of it. Therefore, it is the duty of the regulator, as an agent of the society, to detect and prevent the emergence of such externalities, and in cases where they are inevitable, at least make sure through proper regulation that the sides to the relevant transaction carry the full costs of these externalities, rather than the society.

REGULATORY FAILURE

It is therefore vital for the society to realize that, unless the third condition for Fair Competition, namely the protection of the long-term interests of the whole society, is satisfied through appropriate regulation, even if the other two conditions are fulfilled, and even if the all players on both the supply and the demand sides act within legal boundaries, the welfare of the society will be jeopardized, let alone being maximised.

Needless to say, when one side is the society at large with a diluted attention on any single specific market, while the other side is the beneficiaries of a specific market who concentrate all their efforts to effect the regulator to their own benefit, the job of the regulator is not easy. This *asymmetry of concentration of interests and attention* sometimes causes a regulatory failure where the regulator willingly or unwillingly serves the interests of the concentrated benefit groups at the expense of the society, either through mis-regulation, or a lack of necessary regulation, or its failure in enforcing the existing regulation.

Among the variations of regulatory failure mentioned above, lack of regulation is the best known one, probably because such missing regulation -stemming from the over advertisement of freedom during the latest decades- became too widespread with too strong negative consequences that could not go unnoticed even in the societies with weakened Social Intellect. However, the other two variations that are much less noticed also have equally significant negative consequences. The market may be so mis-regulated that even when all the competitors obey all the regulations, the society can still get harmed. Or, the regulations may not be enforced completely, especially on the strongest players in the market, such that while the Fair Players obey them willingly, the Cheaters do not, and thus the Fair Players eventually lose the competition and get wiped out, at the expense of the society[6].

Fair Competition And The Welfare Of The Society : A Preview

The concept of welfare, and the dynamics of the changes in welfare, will be one of the main themes of Book Three of this series. For now, a preview will suffice to clarify the relation of Fair Competition and the welfare of the society.

In simple terms, the *welfare of the society* is a combined result of *the total wealth of the society* and *the distribution of that wealth within the society* (namely, the inequality within the society). Needless to say, the higher the total wealth and the lower the inequality, the higher the welfare of the society.

FAIR COMPETITION AND ECONOMIC GROWTH

A trivial but significant conclusion of our previous discussion is on the effect of Fair Competition on the economic growth, and thus on the change in the total wealth of the society.

Fair Competition optimizes the conditions on both the supply and the demand sides, and as a consequence, enables the optimal allocation of resources on both. And when the resources are allocated in the optimal manner, the resulting economic growth is maximised.

Therefore, other things being equal, *the more a society approaches Fair Competition, the higher will be its economic growth and the higher will be its accumulated wealth in the long run.*

FAIR COMPETITION AND INEQUALITY

Another significant conclusion of our previous discussion is that, the first condition for Fair Competition, namely fair opportunity for all the competitors in preparation for competition coupled with the chance to compete fairly afterwards, will minimise the artificial inequality created by the lack of such fairness.

Needless to say, there will always be winners and losers under Fair Competition as well, as that is what competition is for. However, as nobody is infinitely better than everybody else at all times, as new competitors arrive the winners will change over time. The accumulated wealth of some competitors may still come out to be higher than others, but they will not be extremely higher than everybody else in the long run. Therefore, although Fair Competition still creates inequality, it is not expected to create Excessive Inequality persistently, but just on the contrary, will annihilate the artificial Excessive Inequality that emerges at its absence.

Therefore, other things being equal, *the more a society approaches Fair Competition, the more the inequality within the society will fall towards acceptable levels.*

FAIR COMPETITION AND THE WELFARE OF THE SOCIETY

Finally, the straightforward but significant conclusion is that, *the more a society approaches Fair Competition, as* the higher will be its total wealth and the lower will be the inequality within the society, *the higher will be its welfare.*

The Ideal Versus The Practical

In practise, it may be difficult to attain the ideal environment for Fair Competition in the way described in this section, especially under the current inadequacy of the Social Intellect of the societies. However, there are always shades of grey between the black and the white, and there are lighter shades versus darker ones. Therefore, without hiding behind excuses based on the difficulty of achieving the ideal, any society, for its own best interest, should try to get as close as possible to Fair Competition if its willing to maximise its welfare in the long run.

Chapter 3

ALTERNATE PATHS TO SUCCESS

3.1   Components Of Success In Competition

Freedom brings competition, and competition serves the development of the society. Competition, however, creates winners and losers, and therefore inequality. Depending on the conditions under which the winners emerge, the resulting inequality may or may not be good for the sustainability of the social order and the maximisation of economic development.

This necessitates the analysis of the alternate paths to success in a competition, to decide whether a path is fair and thus socially acceptable by the society, and whether it enhances the allocation of resources and thus beneficial to the economic growth of the society.

The components of success can be categorized under four main groups.
- Merit
- Excessive Risk Taking, coupled with good luck
- Luck, without excessive risk taking
- Cheating

Within this framework, *Excessive Risk Taking* and *Luck* are considered separately, as being exposed to luck is inevitable, but taking excessive risks is a matter of choice.

Merit is the combination of intelligence (or some special ability), professional education and experience, and hard work.

Excessive Risk Taking, in its simplest form, is undertaking irrational risks such that there is a low chance of ending up at success, and thus success may result if and only if good luck intervenes. Alternatively, it may be defined as taking risks where there may be a higher chance of success over failure, however, in case of failure the risk taker will be completely and irrecoverably ruined.

Luck is the unfair intervention of the randomness in the nature of the universe, that may even stretch to the occurrence of the utterly improbable from time to time.

And *Cheating*, in simple terms, is pursuing unfair or unethical or even illegal competition, the ways of which are only limited by one's imagination.

Among these four main components, although its definition above is the strangest, Luck is actually the only one that is self-explanatory in practice. The other three components will therefore be analysed in detail: Merit and Excessive Risk Taking in the coming sections of this chapter, and Cheating in the next chapter.

3.2   Merit, Calculated Risks And Luck

Merit

Merit can be defined as the combination of intelligence or some special ability, professional education and experience, and hard work.

As the definition starts with intelligence, which is a matter of luck at birth and thus out of one's control (at least until genetic engineering will take care of the lack of it in the future), it is sometimes argued that merit contains a component of luck within itself. This, however, is mostly a convenient excuse to hide the lack of the other components of merit which are within one's control. It is true that, in some cases outstanding-intelligence may be required to achieve extreme-success, and in all cases it helps to perform better, however, it is not needed to become a decent winner.

The most important component of merit is hard work, provided that it focuses on one's areas of comparative advantage with respect to the others in terms of his personal abilities. It starts with personal time and effort invested in education and developing professional expertise, and continues with sustained hard work during one's productive life. Therefore, provided that a fair opportunity for education and employment was available, winning through merit is primarily within the control of the individual, and therefore is fair. By the same token, losing through lack of merit, primarily due to the lack of hard work, again provided that an opportunity for education and employment was available, is also fair. And the most important of all, *both winning and losing through merit, provided that a fair opportunity for education and employment existed, enhances the allocation of resources of the society, by promoting those who deserve to win and eliminating those who deserve to lose.*

Needless to say, in cases where a fair opportunity for education and employment were unavailable, although winning through merit remains to be fair, the verdict for losing through lack of merit becomes vague, as it can not be clear whether the real reason is the lack of hard work or the lack of a fair opportunity. It is true that some people who choose to work hard, still lose due to not having a fair opportunity in education or employment, and thus their loss is not deserved. Moreover, in such cases the society is also penalised as there will be a misallocation of resources. However, it is also true that, many people who become losers, and complain about not being given a fair opportunity in life, would still have failed even if they were given a fair opportunity at the beginning, simply because their failure is due to their lack of hard work, which would not have changed under any condition. In such cases, not only their loss is well deserved, but the allocation of resources within the society is actually enhanced by their loss. Therefore, it is for the best interest of the society to provide a fair opportunity for education and employment, so that individuals will not be able to hide their lack of hard work behind the excuse of a lack of opportunity.

Luck

Some people are simply lucky. They do not work hard, or take excessive risks, or even cheat, but just get the right winds in their sails to push them up. And sometimes the wind pushes them so far up that it requires more than a lifetime to fall back, making their rise seem permanent for practical purposes.

And some people are simply unlucky. However hard they work, whatever they do, the winds against them can be so strong that they may never succeed.

In principle, both winning and losing through pure luck is unfair. In practice, however, winning through good luck is still considered to be fair by the society, seemingly for three reasons. First, there is no easy way of measuring the effect of good luck behind any success. Second, even in principle, there is no unethical or illegal behaviour behind it, as it is totally out of the control of the individual. And finally, everybody wants to keep the hope that one day good luck may find them, and in case that happens, the society would not deny their success - nobody lets their dreams die first.

Still, *from the viewpoint of allocation of resources, both winning and losing through pure luck will cause a misallocation, and thus are not good for the society.*

Unfortunately, the damage done by pure luck is not limited to the misallocation of resources, but spreads further to misguide the society, especially in cases where the society fails to distinguish extreme-good-luck from merit. The simple illustration below reveals why and how that happens.

First, consider the case of Johnny B. Lucky. He wins the national lottery, simply because he bought the ticket with that particular number at that particular lottery date. As his luck is so explicit, nobody suspects of any infinite-wisdom or perfect-vision of Johnny. Nobody asks him to join TV shows or lecture at universities to enlighten the public on how to choose a lottery ticket and find the way to success. Nobody writes a case study on Johnny. Explicit luck in this case brought financial success but not much else. No prestige. No admirers. No followers. No social status. No assumed leadership potential. And all that is natural and rational.

But next consider the case of Freddie B. Lucky. In business, one may sometimes happen to be at the right place at the right time under the right conditions, and then such extreme-good-luck may bring extreme-success. Freddie is such a person with such extreme-good-luck and thus such an extreme-success story. But in his case, the society will think (or be persuaded by Freddie to think) that he has infinite-wisdom and perfect-vision to be at that particular position. As his luck is implicit, the society will naively fail to see the role of extreme-good-luck in his extreme-success. He will be asked to join TV shows or lecture at universities to enlighten the public on how to be so successful in business life. Case studies will be written on Freddie. He will have prestige, admirers, followers, and social status. *And the worst of all, he will be assumed to have the intellectual potential to lead the society.* And *nobody will ask what he could have achieved with his assumed infinite-wisdom and perfect-vision, if he were born at an inconvenient place at an inconvenient time.* His attitude to work, his formation of strategies, his approach to his stakeholders, and anything he does, will be taken to be golden rules for success, *causing further misallocation of resources by those who try to imitate him.*

To cut the long story short, implicit or explicit, extreme-good-luck creates a misallocation of resources and thus harms the welfare of the society.

Merit Versus Luck

The above illustration reveals that misevaluating the winners on good-luck for winning on merit is a major mistake that harms the society in the long run. Similarly, misevaluating the winners on merit for winning on good-luck is also a major mistake with equivalent negative consequences.

Those who choose to compete and win based on merit, may primarily do it for ethical reasons. However, they also expect that, when they win through merit, the appropriate judgement of the society will bring them a deserved recognition coupled with the respect of the society. It is crucial to notice that, the material benefits of success can not be a determinant on their choice, simply because such material benefits will come with all types of success anyway, and probably their magnitude will be the lowest when they are attained through success based on merit under Fair Competition.

When the winners on merit are misjudged by the society as merely being lucky, their motivation will weaken and the society will obviously suffer the natural consequences. The critical question, therefore, is why the society makes such a misjudgement.

The trouble arises from the fact that, very many cases that are complicated but still analysable by the educated professionals, seem to be un-analysable to the society as it lacks the ability to understand such cases. Thus comes the naive logic that the winners should have won on good luck rather than merit.

The society should realise that, in many cases, a professional, based on his merit, can analyse a case much better than the average person and can see the opportunities that others can't, or can avoid the traps that others may fall into, and therefore, may take a rational calculated risk on that case that eventually leads to success. And this success based on merit has nothing to do with good-luck. However, there may also be some other cases which are so complex that they are beyond any expert's merit to analyse, and thus any success in them can really be a matter of good luck. Therefore, the trouble in deciding the source of success still remains for the society, as the society can not differentiate what is a complicated but analysable case (where success may be based on merit) versus what is an un-analysable one even for the professionals (where success can only be based on good luck). At this point comes the need to look for other signs of merit versus luck, in order to make a fair and correct judgement.

Considering the signs of merit, the intelligence of an individual can not be easily determined from the outside, however, the other components of merit, namely professional education and experience, and hard work, can easily be observed by the society. But the real critical distinction comes from the fact that *merit can not suddenly come out of thin air, but rather is accumulated over years, and so is the success attained through merit.* Therefore, *when too much success comes too fast, especially without explicit signs of merit, the society has a valid reason to suspect that a significant component of good-luck is involved.*

In short, when the society fairly judges the winners on merit and rewards them with recognition and respect, it will motivate its members to choose that path, and consequently will serve its own best interest in the long run.

Calculated Risks Versus Excessive Risks

There is no way to achieve any success without taking any risks, and thus, even those aiming to succeed through merit have to take some risks. However, the amount of risk an individual (or a corporation) takes may vary a lot, with different significant consequences, not only for the individual (or for the corporation), but also for the society.

To be able to discuss the different types of risk taking and their consequences, we will split the picture into *Calculated Risks* and *Excessive Risks*, and utilize a few concepts to draw the line in between. Under this distinction, *winning through Merit naturally requires taking calculated risks, but necessitates avoiding excessive risks.*

CALCULATED RISKS

For an action to be qualified as calculated risk taking, two conditions have to be met simultaneously. First, in simple terms, the expectation of success must dominate the expectation of failure. Second, the risk taker (the individual or the corporation) must have enough risk taking capacity, such that, in case of failure, the whole burden must be totally borne by the risk taker, preferably without ruining himself. Otherwise, the action is considered to be excessive risk taking.

EXPECTED OUTCOMES

Let us start with the first condition.

When an individual (or a corporation) takes an action, there are many possible outcomes, with different probabilities, and with different values for that individual (or corporation). Conceptually, the probability-weighted average of the values of all these possible outcomes defines the Expected Outcome of that action for the risk taker.

For the simplicity of our analysis, we will assume that there are only two outcomes, one positive and one negative. Then, we can define:

Expected Outcome =
  (Probability of positive outcome)*(Value of positive outcome)
    + (Probability of negative outcome)*(Value of negative outcome)

To illustrate, consider a simple case of financial investment. Assume that there are two available projects as given below (whether each $1 represents $10.000 for an individual, or $ 1 billion for a corporation does not change the analysis), where a positive $ value corresponds to a profit, and a negative $ value corresponds to a loss.

Project A:
Positive outcome :   +$20 with a probability of 60%
Negative outcome :   -$40 with a probability of 40%
Expected Outcome : 60%*($20) + 40%*(-$40) = -$4.00

Project B:
Positive outcome :   +$15 with a probability of 65%
Negative outcome :   -$10 with a probability of 35%

Expected Outcome : 65%*($15) + 35%*(-$10) = $6.25

The expected outcome of Project A is negative (a loss of $4.00), while that of Project B is positive (a profit of $6.25). Therefore, in principle, an investor that takes calculated risks will only accept Project B, and avoid Project A.

In principle, if a risk taker is merited and takes only calculated risks, his path to success should be clear and open. In practise, however, luck is always there to play its part, especially in the short run. In the illustration above, the calculated-risk taker may still face a loss with Project B, as there is a 35% chance of losing. Similarly, an investor who for some reason (like miscalculating the expected outcome) has taken Project A, may still win, as there is a 60% chance of winning. In practise, therefore, *within the scope of a single case, a positive outcome does not necessarily justify the correctness of the initial choice, and similarly, a negative outcome does not mean that the initial decision was wrong.*

The important fact, however, is that, even if luck may play a role in the short run and bring out unexpected results, when similar actions are repeated for many times, as a natural rule of statistics, those sequences made up of actions with positive expected outcomes will always cumulate to give a net positive final result, and vice versa. Therefore, *in the long run, those who take calculated risks will definitely succeed and this will have nothing to do with good luck,* while, *those taking excessive risks will definitely fail and again this will have nothing to do with bad luck.*

It is crucial to observe that, for the dynamics of statistics to work and enable the risk taker to attain long-term-success-based-on-merit-independent-of-luck, he should be able to repeat such actions-based-on-calculated-risks again and again. However, if a single loss will burn out all his fuel and take him out of the market, such dynamics will have no chance to work, and thus making decisions based on positive expected outcomes will have no practical use. And this brings us to the second condition regarding risk taking capacity.

RISK TAKING CAPACITY

Risk taking capacity is simply the ability to *afford the most negative outcome* that may result from taking a certain risky action, without ruining the risk-taker, such that he will be able to take further calculated risks later on.

This definition clarifies two significant issues. First, risk taking capacity is not effected by the *probability* of the most negative outcome. However low the probability may be, as long as it is above zero, the most negative outcome may get realized and the risk-taker may have to bear the consequence. And second, risk taking capacity is directly related to the risk-taker and not to the risky action. This is simply because, the potential most negative outcome of a risky action may be affordable by one risk-taker while it may totally ruin some other. Therefore, assuming a positive expected outcome, that risky action may be a calculated risk for the first risk-taker, while it is an excessive risk for the other one.

To illustrate, consider the case below:

Project C, with an Expected Outcome = %95*(+10) + %5*(-50) = 7

Project D, with an Expected Outcome = %95*(+100) + %5*(-500) = 70

In this case, both projects have a positive expected outcome and for both the probability of the worst case is low (%5). However, the magnitude of the worst possible outcome of project D (-500) is much worse than that of C (-50).

For a risk-taker who can easily handle a loss of (-500) if it materializes, undertaking both projects will be calculated risk taking, and he will most probably choose to take Project D, as its expected outcome is much higher. However, for another risk-taker who can afford the potential loss in project C, but will not be able to survive the huge potential loss in project D, project D classifies as excessive risk taking, and thus he can only undertake project C as a calculated risk.

To summarize, if the magnitude of the potential most negative outcome is too big compared to a risk-taker's capacity, such that he will not have further chances to repeat calculated risk taking strategies in case the worst outcome hits, then he should avoid taking that risky action even if the expected outcome of the action is positive. Therefore, in practise, the magnitude of the most negative outcome relative to the capacity of the risk-taker is the crucial issue, independent of the probability of that outcome. If the risk-taker can not survive the worst outcome, then that action classifies as excessive risk taking for him[7].

THE BOTTOM LINE

When an individual (or a corporation) takes calculated-risks-within-his-risk-taking-capacity to accompany merit, then success in the long run through such calculated risk taking is fair, and helps to optimise the allocation of resources within the society.

3.3 Excessive Risk Taking

Why Does Anyone Take Excessive Risks?

When we have explained the rationality of the case with calculated risk taking in the previous section, we have also revealed the irrationality[8] of taking excessive risks.

In cases where the expected outcome of an action is negative, such risk taking attitude will surely end up at a cumulative loss when repeated in the long run – even if the risk taker has enough risk taking capacity[9]. Therefore, the primary reason why anyone takes actions with negative expected outcomes is that, the risk taker is not merited enough to see the risks, as will be discussed in the next sub-section.

In other cases of excessive risk taking, where the risk taker is quite merited and clearly knows that (while the expected outcome is positive) the most negative potential outcome is beyond his risk taking capacity, but still chooses to take that action, there are reasons behind the curtain that changes the nature of the game.

One such reason is that the risk taker can somehow transfer most of the loss of the potential negative outcome to the society, and thus practically decreases the magnitude of the potential loss (such that it easily fits within his risk taking capacity) - as will be discussed in the following sub-section.

Another reason is that the probability of the potential negative outcome is practically nullified, as the game is rigged and the outcome is pre-fixed based on the cheating of the risk taker, most probably in cooperation with some corrupt agents - as will be discussed in the next chapter.

When One Fails To See The Risks

Consider a case of driving a motorcycle at 300 km/hr to break a speed record. For someone with no special ability to drive a motorcycle, the probability of death on trial is almost 100%, thus, no rational person who is aware of the risk of driving a motorcycle at such high speeds will take such a risk. Now consider some guy with a special ability to drive a motorcycle, for whom the risk of death falls to 75% and therefore who may succeed to break the record with a 25% chance. The crucial point here is that, for any rational person who is aware that there is a 75% risk of death, in spite of having a special ability, it still does not make sense to take such a risk. Once in a while, however, people without the awareness of that 75% risk of death, but with that special ability, will come along and try to break the record, and sooner or later somebody will naturally succeed, as there is a 25% probability of success for those with that special ability. But that success will be achieved at the expense of those who tried and failed.

Even though a special ability can be considered as a sub-component of merit, as long as it is not accompanied by other sub-components like intelligence and rationality, but rather contradicts with them, it can not alone qualify as a sign of merit. To be more precise, winning through merit necessitates rationality-stemming-from-intelligence, and therefore can not include excessive risk taking which is irrational. Thus, the success in this illustration, which is based on courage-stemming-from-ignorance, in addition to the special ability, can not be considered to be based on merit, but just on excessive risk taking and accompanying good luck.

LACK OF MERIT

Remember the definition

Expected Outcome =
(Probability of positive outcome)*(Value of positive outcome)
+ (Probability of negative outcome)*(Value of negative outcome)

where, for a decision based on merit, the Expected Outcome must be positive.

The motorcycle illustration above is a case with a potential extremely negative outcome (namely, death) with a high probability (75% even for those with that special ability), and thus its expected outcome is terribly negative, making it an exaggerated case of excessive risk taking. In practise, such exaggerated cases may be rare, but cases of taking excessive risks due to lack of merit are common.

The lack of merit in such cases primarily stems from either the lack of intellect or ability, or the lack of education and experience, or both. In either case, the risk taker fails to properly assess the probabilities and the magnitudes of the components of expected outcome, such that he ends up with a misleading positive expectation, while a correct assessment would have given a negative expected outcome. Thus, even though the risk taker may be willing to take only calculated risks, based on his mistake in the analysis, he may unintentionally take an excessive risk.

POSITIVITY BIAS

The mistakes in the assessment of expected outcome does not only arise out of lack of merit as defined above, but sometimes out of emotional preferences for a particular action that may cloud objective thinking, even in rational risk takers. This is called a *positivity bias* in risk assessment.

Under positivity bias, the risk taker tends to assume either the probability of the potential positive outcome to be much higher than it actually is (thus, assumes the probability of the potential negative outcome much lower than it actually is), and/or the magnitude of the potential positive outcome to be much higher than it actually is, and/or the magnitude of the potential negative outcome to be much lower than it actually is.

For a simple illustration, assume

Objective Expected Outcome = $60\%*(+10) + 40\%*(-20) = -2$

But under the influence of the positivity bias, the risk taker unknowingly assumes

Biased Expected Outcome = $70\%*(+15) + 30\%*(-15) = +6$

In this case, although an objective assessment would reveal that taking this action will be excessive risk taking, the biased assessment misguides the risk taker to see a case of well calculated risk. Thus, positivity bias leads to excessive risk taking without being aware of it.

The discrepancy between the misbelief and the reality is the result of the positivity bias. This phenomenon of *feelings distorting reality*, such that one desires a possible potential outcome too much to the point of blurring his rationality, is quite common in both economics and politics.

And *when excessive risks are taken in economics and politics under the influence of positivity bias, there will naturally be a clear misallocation of resources. Avoiding such bias, however, is easy to say but difficult to achieve, simply because the only way to avoid falling into this bias is having a high level of Social Intellect which unfortunately is not a widespread phenomenon even in the economically advanced western societies.*

BLINDED BY GREED

Needless to say, the strongest emotion that creates a positivity bias is greed.

A common case of excessive risk taking in economics, based on the misguidance of greed, can be observed at times of high economic growth. High growth, which never lasts forever, also never fails to trigger the animal spirits in many individuals and corporations. At times of high growth, when whatever one does will probably bring success and growth and profits, many individuals and corporations start to take excessive risks based on biased calculations to maximise their benefits, forcing their rivals to do the same in order to be able to stay in the game. And success comes in the short-term. Egos boost. It suddenly appears clear to everyone that high growth is here to stay this time, although it never ever did in the past. A few unlucky managers who may choose to think rationally and try to stay at the side lines are immediately kicked out of the game, as they are diagnosed with the fatal illness of missing guts or brains. Only some individuals with brains but without guts, who are lucky enough to be responsible only to their own selves, may have the luxury to stay on the side lines. The rest maximise their risks through increasing leverage (debts) and heavily investing for the very long-term, as if the long-term is forecastable. The society admires and cherishes those who miss no chance to maximise growth in the short run through undertaking any risks they may find around. Then, as it always happened in the past, the tide suddenly turns for some reason that was completely unforecastable, at least from the viewpoint of the risk takers, until it came out. Everybody enters a state of shock for history simply repeating itself, again. Excessive risks turn sour, short-term profits turn to heavy losses, corporations and individual lives collapse, resources are wasted, and the society (including the few individuals without guts who stayed put, as there is no escape from others' sins) has no chance but to take over the losses and bear the burden, as it always happened in the past. Instability and volatility skyrockets. The welfare of the society is heavily harmed for the long-term. Another story of greed is over, till the next time it comes around[10].

EXCESSIVE RISK TAKING: THE INNOCENTS AND THE CHEATERS

Excessive Risk Taking based on the miscalculation of risks naturally ends in a loss most of the times. However, it may also end up in success once in a while by the help of extreme good luck. Unfortunately, independent of the end result, it *causes a misallocation of resources*.

Such Excessive Risk Taking behaviour is not deliberate cheating as it is primarily based on an innocent miscalculation. But unfortunately, its consequence is similar to that of cheating: a decrease in the welfare of the society in the long run.

And then there is the other case where excessive risks are taken based on the fact that any potential loss will be transferred to somebody else – who happens to be the society most of the times, and that is exactly cheating.

When One Can Avoid Bearing The Burden Of The Loss

In Excessive Risk Taking, failure to see the risks is just one part of the story. In many cases, what heavily fuels excessive risk taking is having the means to keep any potential profits to one's own self while to shift any potential losses to somebody else, through many advanced structures, a phenomenon known as the "heads I win, tails you lose" approach in the financial jargon.

These advanced structures serve their purposes in the best possible way when the eventual loss-bearing side happens to be the society, as the society is mostly incapable of protecting its own interests against such fine-tuned structures due to its lack of social awareness. Thus, such structures that shift the burden of losses to the society at times of failure are common in both economics and politics. In this sub-section we will focus on the economics part, and in later chapters, on politics.

To get a feeling of how the system motivates Excessive Risk Taking and how the resulting losses flow through these structures to eventually reach the society, it will suffice to review the very basics of the corporate and financial sectors.

THE LIMITED LIABILITY COMPANY

The *limited liability company*, a legal structure where the liability of the company is limited by its capital, and thus the liability of the shareholders and the debtholders are limited by the capital they put in the company, is at the heart of the current economic system and is considered to be one of the great inventions of capitalism. In its basic form, both shareholders and debtholders (banks, bondholders, or any other lenders) supply financial resources, and the managers make the risk taking decisions. At the end of the day, first the debtholders get paid back, either through the profits or the capital supplied by the shareholders, and whatever is left - if any- belongs to the shareholders. This simple structure seems to be fool proof on the surface, at least in the sense that the shareholders need to make sure that the debtholders are paid back in full, so that the shareholders can get something themselves. However, as the liability of the shareholders is limited with the amount of capital they put in, the debtholders themselves are expected to be cautious enough to watch the risk taking attitude of the company, and not to lend in case the management starts to take excessive risks that may endanger the receivables of the debtholders. Finally, in case they fail the shareholders, the managers will lose their jobs. It all seems that calculated risk taking is for the best interest of all the parties involved.

THE TROUBLE WITH THE MANAGERS

As discussed in detail in Book One, managers act as the agents of the shareholders and make the risk taking decisions on their behalf. To align the interests of the managers with those of the shareholders, advanced compensation systems where managers are heavily rewarded for their success are developed on a company basis. However, all these compensation systems have one attitude in common: they evaluate and reward short-term performances, and can never take these rewards back – independent of what happens in the long-term. And the short-term, whether it is a year or a couple of years, is a period much less than the lifetime of the company.

Remember that, the expected outcome calculations on which risk taking decisions are based, are made before any action is taken, but the eventual outcome is realised much later in the future. Keeping this time span in mind, a manager waits for an appropriate time for positive external economic conditions, and then takes excessive risks for the company such that some very positive results will be obtained in the shorter run, at the expense of a potential catastrophic outcome in the long run. In the short run, either high risks return temporary high profits, or heavy investments create an illusion of increased future prospects of the company in the eyes of the financial analysts and shareholders, all increasing the share price of the company. As most of the financial compensation of the managers are tied to the short-term share price of the company, the financial rewards of the manager skyrockets in the short run. And what happens in the long run varies. One possibility is that, the manager may simply leave the company sometime before the catastrophic outcome materializes, with all his past rewards and without any obligation to payback any of them, leaving the eventual trouble to other managers. In rare cases, it is possible that the catastrophic outcome may arrive sooner than even the manager expects, thus before he has a chance to leave, but still all he loses is his job, but not the accumulated past rewards. And in practise, most managers have legal agreements that supply a golden parachute in case they are fired, thus, if the company is kept alive through injection of new capital, they will also get a final huge additional reward for their failure. Another possibility is that, if the manager is lucky, the catastrophic outcome materializes during an economy-wide crisis. In this case, as any individual manager can not be held accountable for such a wide spread crisis (the great excuse of the managers, as if the occurrence of such crises once in a while is an unimaginable phenomenon), the manager may even save his job in case the company is kept alive, for the sake of all the glorious days he had in the past, coupled with the naive expectation that he may have success again in the future, namely when market conditions improve to bring success naturally.

In short, when the managers can heavily benefit from the temporary positive outcomes in the short run, but are only minimally effected by any potential negative outcome in the long run (as they leave the burden of that loss to the company), they naturally tend to take excessive risks for the company to boost short-term positive outcomes. The remedy for this problem is then clear: the shareholders should not only focus on the short-term outcomes, but must also take into consideration the amount and type of risks taken by the managers to achieve those outcomes[11].

The real issue, however, is whether the shareholders are really willing the managers to take only calculated risks, or do they actually prefer excessive risk taking for reasons of their own.

THE TROUBLE WITH THE SHAREHOLDERS

The limited liability structure of a company actually motivates taking risky action coupled with heavy borrowing (called *high leverage* in the jargon) for an obvious reason: if the company succeeds, the shareholders will get the lion's share of the profits, but if the company fails, the debtholders will bear most of the loss. This is simply because, when the company fails, shareholders lose the capital they have put in while debtholders may lose all the credit they have given, and this will be terribly unfair for the debtholders as their loss happens to be much more than that of the shareholders in highly leveraged companies. Therefore, borrowing heavily is within the logic of the limited liability company – a logic that stands for "heads the shareholders win, tails the debtholders lose".

As a simple illustration, consider the cases below. In both cases, the company has its own capital of $100 paid by the shareholders. It can borrow further from a bank (the debtholder) and invest in a project. Assume that the probability of success of the project is 90% in both cases.

In the first case, the company takes a low-risk project and prefers low leverage. It borrows $100 from the bank. Assume that the interest rate charged by the bank is for low risk projects is 5%. It invests in a project such that in case of success, the project pays 35% on the capital invested, and, in case of failure, loses 20% on the capital invested. If the project fails, the company loses $40 (ends up with $160) and after paying pack $105 to the bank (including interest), the shareholders are left with $55. Thus, the shareholders take a loss, but the company survives. If the project succeeds, the company earns $70 (ends up with $270), and after paying pack $105 to the bank (including interest), the shareholders are left with $165, a 65% return on the initial capital they have invested.

As the *project* has a positive expected outcome [90%*(35%) + 10%* (-20%) = 29.5%], and the potential loss [-$45] of the shareholders after paying interest is within the risk taking capacity of the *shareholders' equity* ($100), this is a calculated risk taking behaviour for the *company*.

Therefore, all this is fine, except that the greed of the shareholders (and the managers) is left unsatisfied. Thus, the next case will present further risk taking.

In this second case, the company takes a risky project and works with a higher leverage. In case of success, the risky project pays 60% on the capital invested, but in case of failure loses all the capital invested (i.e. returns -100%). Assume that the interest rate charged by the bank is for highly leveraged risky projects is 20%. The company borrows $300 from the bank and invests all $400. If the project fails, it loses all the investment, leaving the shareholders with a loss of $100, and the bank with a loss of $300. If the project succeeds, the company earns $240 (ends up with $640), and after paying pack $360 to the bank (including interest), the shareholders are left with $280, a return of 180% on their initial investment.

Notice that the *risky project* still has a positive expected outcome [90%*(60%) + 10%*(-100%) = 44%]. However, the potential loss [-$460, including the interest liability to the bank] of the shareholders is way above the risk taking capacity of the *shareholders' equity* ($100), making this an excessive risk taking behaviour for the *company*. Thus, in case of failure, as the liability of the shareholders is limited by their capital ($100), the rest of the loss is transferred to the bank.

The simple question -with the obvious answer- is, which case would the shareholders prefer?

For the shareholders, the expected outcomes of these two cases are (in terms of the return on initial capital) :

Exp. outcome for *shareholders* (case 1) = 10%*(-45%) + 90%*(65%) = 54%

Exp. outcome for *shareholders* (case 2) = 10%*(-100%) + 90%*(180%) = 152%

It is clear from this simple illustration that, as long as the bank can somehow be persuaded to lend $300 to the risky project, the shareholders (and the manager, as he shares some of the profit through his compensation system) would choose to take the risky project with a high leverage, to increase the overall risk as much as possible. The high expected outcome of excessive risk taking behaviour for the shareholders is simply the result of the transfer of the potential extra loss to the bank in case of failure, while keeping the potential extra profit to themselves in case of success.

This situation, which may be called "heads the shareholders (and managers) win, tails the debtholders lose", reveals why the shareholders may actually prefer excessive risk taking *for the company*, with risky projects and high leverage.

The crucial observation here is that, the second case is excessive risk taking for the *company*, as potential failure will wipe out its shareholders' equity, but it is *not* excessive-risk taking for the *shareholders*, simply because, from their viewpoint, it satisfies both of the conditions for calculated risk taking. First, the expected outcome for the shareholders is positive (152% in the illustration), and actually way above that of the company (44% in the illustration) due to the high leverage. And second, a potential failure will only wipe out the initial capital supplied by the shareholders, which probably is only a fraction of their overall capital (rest of which is invested elsewhere, diversified into other types of assets), and thus losing their initial capital is easily within the risk taking capacity of the shareholders. In other words, the risk taking capacity of the *shareholders' equity in the company* (namely $100 in the illustration above), is practically way below the risk taking capacity of the *shareholders own capital* which is isolated from the liabilities of the company due to the limited liability nature of the company. This is the catch that enables the transfer of most of the loss to the bank and thus skyrockets the expected outcome for the shareholders in the second case.

The bottom line is that, as shown in the illustration, the *shareholders of the company* prefer the second case with the risky project and high leverage, simply because, how spectacularly the company fails does not matter as long as it fails - as their loss is limited by their capital-, but how spectacularly a company succeeds makes all the difference in terms of maximising their potential profits.

Therefore, the only remaining question is, why has the bank accepted to lend to the risky project above with that high leverage? Not out of lack of merit, of course.

THE TROUBLE WITH THE DEBTHOLDERS OF THE COMPANY

The bank, as the debtholder in the illustration above, is also a limited liability company with its own managers and shareholders, and debtholders.

The story with its managers, therefore, is similar to that of any other company: in line with their short-term oriented compensation schemes, bank managers tend to take high risks for the bank such that some very positive results will be obtained in the shorter run, at the expense of a potential major negative outcome in the longer run. And again, the real issue is whether the *shareholders of the bank* prefer the bank managers to lend to risky projects, for reasons of their own.

Returning to the illustration above, the low-risk (case 1) and the high-risk (case 2) projects have different expected outcomes for the bank:
Exp. outcome of project for the bank (case 1) = 100%*(5%) = 5%
Exp. outcome of project for the bank (case 2) = 10%*(-100%) + 90%*(20%) = 8%

The expected outcome is positive for both cases, and naturally higher for the risky project, thus motivating the bank to prefer the risky one from that viewpoint. However, to decide whether lending to the risky project creates an excessive risk to the bank, we need to consider the *risk taking capacity of the bank*.

A bank always distributes its lending (and thus the risks it takes) among many different borrowers in more or less equal amounts. This ensures that any single loss arising from a failed credit will remain way below the risk taking capacity of the bank, creating no trouble at all on an individual basis. And when banks diversify their risks to many companies in this manner, even if each project they lend to is risky by itself, the eventual outcomes of those risky projects will not be correlated with each other *under normal conditions,* and thus, on the aggregate all these company-specific risks are nullified. What this practically means is that, even if some of the borrowers default, the high revenue from the rest will create an overall profit that makes it worth to take such risks in aggregate. Therefore, in our illustration, the bank expects to get an aggregate return of 8% on its lending to such risky projects in the long run.

To clarify, therefore, lending to companies that take excessive risks is *not* an excessive risk taking behaviour *for the bank*, but on the contrary, it qualifies as a calculated risk taking approach for the bank, since both the expected outcome for the bank is positive, and the potential losses are minimised through diversification and thus do not exceed the risk taking capacity of the bank *under normal conditions*.

As a result of such diversification and resulting nullification of company-specific risks, the bank seems to have a secure structure, and thus works under high leverage itself. Actually, the leverages of the banks (or the financial sector in general) are practically much higher than those of non-financial companies, and may practically reach 1-to-10 or higher. The debtholders of the banks vary from individual or corporate depositors to other banks or financial institutions.

The expected return of the *shareholders of the bank* can be calculated in the same way that those of the shareholders of the company are calculated. However, the extremely leveraged structure of the bank will amplify the difference between lending to companies that take calculated risks versus lending to companies that take excessive risks.

To continue the illustration, assume that the bank has $1.000 of shareholders' equity, and $9.000 of debtholders' deposit, where the debtholders demand 4% interest as the bank itself has a secure structure. Then, the calculations[12] reveal that *when the bank lends to companies that all take calculated risks (case 1 in the illustration) the expected outcome for the shareholders of the bank is 14%, but when the bank lends to companies that all take excessive risks (case 2 in the illustration) the expected outcome for the shareholders of the bank is 48%. Therefore, the shareholders of the bank will definitely prefer the bank managers to lend to companies that take excessive risks.*

And as explained above, even when the banks extend credits to risky projects or companies, everything works fine for the bank, and for its shareholders, and for its debtholders under normal conditions. That is, until an economy-wide crisis hits.

The trouble with economy-wide crises is that, it is impossible to forecast their timing, but they have this habit of coming around every 10 to 20 years. And they significantly effect all the companies in all sectors in a negative way. This in turn, increases the probability of failure of the risky projects in all sectors and companies.

In our illustration, this may mean that the probability of loss for the risky projects has now risen from 10% to 30%. Then, the expected outcome for the bank regarding its risky credits becomes:

Expected outcome for bank (case 2) = 30%*(-100%) + 70%*(20%) = -16%

And now the bank will face a loss of 16% on aggregate on its credits. However, due to its high leverage, only 10% of its credits are financed by the shareholders of the bank, and thus the remaining loss have to taken by the *bank's debtholders*. In other words, the bank will have to default on some of its own liabilities.

The financial sector, however, is built on trust. When even one bank defaults, the debtholders of all the other banks, especially the private depositors, may panic and try to take back their deposits. This is what is known as a banking-run in the jargon, meaning a sudden withdrawal of funds from the banking system. However, banks practically tie most of their deposits to relatively longer term credits, and thus, in case of a banking-run, will face a liquidity crisis, even if they are solvent[13], and thus will fail to pay back deposits, fuelling the panic further. And this dynamic may quickly evolve into a systematic failure of the financial sector, unless immediate counter action is taken.

The critical difference here is that, unlike any corporate sector, the financial sector is at the heart of the whole economy. Therefore, even though a society may let one particular corporate sector to fail on its own for whatever reason, no society can let its finance sector collapse. When the financial sector comes to the edge of collapsing, as it happened in the 2008 crisis, the society, through the state, has to step in by whatever means necessary and make sure that the financial sector survives - even though some of its shareholders may lose some or all of their capital in the process[14]. This means that the losses of the financial sector will be borne by the state, through some sort of injection of fresh capital to the financial sector, which in turn means that these losses will eventually be paid by the society through a variety of direct and indirect taxes.

Therefore, *what seems to be a rational calculated risk taking approach for the financial sector at regular times, evolves into excessive risk taking behaviour at times of economy-wide crises, as the potential loss from risky credits rise above the risk taking capacity of the banks.* Moreover, *due to the nature of the sector and the debtholders of the banks, the resulting losses are eventually transferred to the society.* Therefore, when the possibility of economy-wide crises is taken into account, in our jargon, such excessive risk taking behaviour of the financial sector can be described as "heads the shareholders of the financial institutions win, tails the society lose".

In short, under such excessive risk taking behaviour throughout the whole system, when an economy-wide crisis hits, as it always does at some point in time, huge losses start to arise from the corporate sector, then get transferred to the financial sector, and eventually, conveniently end up on the shoulders of the society.

TOO BIG TO FAIL?

We have discussed that due to its unique and indispensable status in the economy, the financial sector can not be sacrificed at times of crises. Unfortunately, it is not the only sector that the society finds itself obliged to save, but there are many other sectors that the society can not sacrifice and thus have to compensate for their losses at times of crises. Thus, huge losses of some corporate sectors may directly end up on the shoulders of the society as well.

The criteria for selecting the sectors to be saved by the society, in case the need arises, is ambiguous. One obvious criterion can be the sectors that are strategically critical for the survival of the society. But the more practical criterion is the economic size of the sector, as the bigger its size, the bigger is the direct and indirect impacts of its failure on the economy. This introduced the concept of too-big-to-fail-(company) in the jargon, which unfortunately is misleading, as it is understood to mean that only the major corporations that are monopolies or parts of oligopolies will have to be saved by the society. The proper term should have been *too-important-to-sacrifice-(sector)*, which clarifies that deserving to be saved by the society requires a sector to be important in aggregate, rather than being big in size on an individual company basis.

To illustrate the difference, when the too-big-to-fail-(company) concept is used, an immediate cure seems to be dividing and scaling down major corporations such that neither remain to be too-big-to-fail and each can be sacrificed individually. The catch here is that, unless they change their risk taking attitude, at times of economy-wide crises, they will fail all together as a sector, and the society will again have to save them. Therefore, scaling down major risky companies to smaller risky ones is not a solution, unless the risks taken by the sector in aggregate is scaled down.

The too-important-to-sacrifice phenomenon can also arise from a wide spread risk taking behaviour shared by many individuals in a society.

Even when individuals in a society act on their own without any explicit coordination, if very many of them share a systematic excessive risk taking behaviour, then when an economy-wide crisis hits they will collectively become too-important-to-sacrifice on a social basis, necessitating the rest of the society to pay for the loss they have faced. A well known example is the case when many individuals borrowed heavily and invested in housing based on a bet on rising prices, and then faced the mortgage crisis in 2008. The risk takers in such cases may not initially be aware of the possibility of transferring their potential losses to the society, and thus may be naïve and innocent, meaning that they have taken those risks simply because they lacked the merit to prevent them from taking such excessive risks, but still the society pays for their mistakes following the crisis. Therefore, as discussed in Book One of this series, it will be for the best interest of the society to increase the Social Intellect of all its members as much as possible as soon as possible.

Before proceeding further, it is necessary to make a vital observation: *the real solution for the prevention of the transfer of all sorts of losses mentioned in this sub-section* (those of the financial sector, the too-important-to-sacrifice corporate sector, and the innocent individuals) *to the shoulders of the society, is enacting and enforcing appropriate laws and regulations to prevent any type and size of participant in the economy from taking excessive risks in the first place.*

THE CASE OF MORAL HAZARD

Consider the cars produced decades ago. They were much less safe than those of our day, but the drivers of those cars used to drive much slower too, knowing the risks involved. As technology developed, much safer cars are produced, but now drivers are driving ever faster, counting on the protection provided by the advanced technology. As a result, they eventually find out the limits where even the new technology can not protect them anymore, and accidents, even fatal ones, continue to exist. Therefore, as long as the drivers take on more risks knowing that there is more protection for them when they face accidents, neither the traffic will be safer, nor all the efforts and expenses made to improve the safety of the cars will be of any use. The society ends up at the same danger level, if not worse. This is just a simple illustration of moral hazard.

And cases of moral hazard, motivating excessive risk taking behaviour, are common in economics.

At times of economy-wide crises, the interventions of the Central Banks through changes in their monetary policies and/or the Governments through changes in their financial policies are common, as both are believed to limit the potential damages of crises.

For instance, in our illustration above, such interventions may prevent the chances of the loss of the bank regarding its risky credits from rising all the way to 30%, but just rise a little to 15%. And then the expected outcome for the bank becomes

Expected outcome for bank (case 2) = 15%*(-100%) + 85%*(20%) = +2%

Thus, in spite of the economy-wide crisis, the bank survives and only experiences a fall in profitability. And given this virtual insurance against failure, the Banks will lend more to risky projects, and companies can easily fund risky projects, and thus risky projects will spread further to all markets and companies.

Therefore, from an economic perspective, *when the risk takers in an economy (the managers and the shareholders of both the companies and the financial institutions) know that, at times of economy-wide crises, the state institutions will intervene utilizing the resources of the society, and thus will transfer the burden of the potential losses to the society, they tend to take on higher risks with their businesses*, introducing moral hazard to economics.

Moreover, as discussed before, both the shareholders of the companies and the banks usually diversify their own investments to many different types of assets, including some low-risk and even risk-free ones, to protect themselves from economy-wide crises as much as possible. However, they may not choose to do so if they feel that the state intervention will limit the potential damages of the economy-wide crises. Thus, they may direct more of their own capital to risk taking companies, or to banks who lend to risk taking companies, increasing the riskiness of their own investment portfolios, which in turn creates more capital for risk taking activity and thus increases the overall risk in the system. And this in turn, will further rise the burden of the loss to the society in cases of economy-wide crises.

At first sight, the interventions of Central Banks and/or Governments are believed to be valuable stabilizers at times of economy-wide crises, and this belief definitely has some truth in it. However, such belief, also creates an expectation of intervention during any economy-wide crisis in the future, and motivates the risk takers to significantly amplify the risks they take. Therefore, while on the one hand the interventions of Central Banks and Governments prevent the spread of such crises and stabilise the economy, on the other hand they cause amplified risk taking before any potential crisis, eventually wiping out a significant portion of the value they create for the society in the long run. In other words, such expected interventions may be the devil in disguise, as they create a moral hazard problem that initiates and amplifies a crisis in the first place, by motivating excessive risk taking behaviour.

Therefore, *for such interventions by the state institutions to create significant value for the society in the long run, without being neutralised by the moral hazard they may cause, the risk taking behaviour of both the companies and the financial institutions has to be kept within rational boundaries through enacting and enforcing appropriate laws and regulations.*

THE MISERY OF THE RATIONAL RISK TAKER

When many individuals in a society take excessive risks (by themselves, or through the companies and the financial institutions they own or manage), *and eventually face a loss and pass that loss to the society, each member of the society will have to pay for these losses through a variety of direct and indirect taxes* – as will be discussed in Book Three of this series. Therefore, *even those members of the society who stayed rational and avoided excessive risks will be sharing the losses of those who did not.*

This observation clarifies that, *the freedom of each member of a society to take risks has to be limited by the rights of the other members of the society not to share the potential loss resulting from those risks.* Consequently, *the rational calculated- risk takers in a society have the right to demand the limitation of risks borne by the excessive risk takers, through the enaction and enforcement of appropriate laws and regulations.*

And enacting and enforcing such laws and regulations is a political process, and political processes can work fine if and only if the Social Intellect of the society is adequate. And, as discussed in Book One, all societies have trouble on that front.

IN CONCLUSION

In cases where any potential profits are kept by the risk taker while any potential losses are transferred to the others, and mostly to the society (and this is practically known by the risk taker before the risk is taken, such that the amount of risk taken is amplified because of this asymmetry), *Excessive Risk Taking is virtually equivalent to cheating against the society.*

And needless to say, *such Excessive Risk Taking is unfair and causes a significant misallocation of resources* that decreases the growth rate of the economy.

Any society with adequate Social Intellect would therefore protect itself against such cheating-in-disguise through proper lawmaking and regulation. Those who would like to take such excessive risks usually argue that limitation of excessive risk taking behaviour through regulations may slow down the economic growth in the short-term, implicitly assuming very positive economic conditions. But, economic conditions do not stay positive forever, and when they turn negative, the emerging major losses that are conveniently transferred to the society result in a major misallocation of resources that will definitely harm the economic growth on a larger scale. In the long-term, therefore, avoidance of major transfers of losses to the society, in addition to the prevention of misallocation of resources, will bring out a much higher rate of economic growth. Moreover, when the enaction and enforcement of proper regulations limit excessive risk taking behaviour, the need for the intervention of the Central Banks and Governments at times of economy-wide crises will also be eliminated or at least minimised, and thus cases of moral hazard will be prevented.

3.4 The Strange Case of Extreme-Success

Achieving success is the natural main goal of all competitors in any competition, and is the driving force behind the economic development of the society. However, for the optimisation of the allocation of resources in an economy and the maximisation of the welfare of the society, success has to be obtained in an environment of Fair Competition, mainly through the utilisation of merit. And under Fair Competition, the level of success any competitor can achieve relative to the others practically remain within rational boundaries, as no one is infinitely more merited than all the others.

Therefore, if the winner of a competition absolutely crashed the rest of the competitors and achieved extreme-success, then the fairness of that competition and the optimisation of the allocation of resources are quite suspicious. A further analysis of extreme-success is therefore necessary.

EXTREME-SUCCESS AND EXCESSIVE RISK TAKING

Extreme-success may come as a result of unknowingly taking excessive risks and simultaneously facing extreme-good-luck. Or, it may come from deliberately taking excessive risks based on the fact that any potential losses can and will be transferred to others, including the society. In both cases, as explained before, the resulting extreme-success causes a misallocation of resources.

EXTREME-SUCCESS, MERIT AND LUCK

To analyse the relation of extreme-success with merit and luck, assume that there is neither any excessive risk taking nor any cheating, but just merit and luck as the determinants of success.

In principle, it is possible that extreme-success is a result of superior-merit (i.e. with superior wisdom and vision as additional ingredients) without much contribution of good luck. However, *success-based-only-on-superior-merit has practical limits in a competitive environment.* And *those limits are definitely lower and stay within rational boundaries when there is Fair Competition, as no one is the one-and-only person with superior-merit in any market or society.*

Extreme-success, therefore, most probably stems from extreme-good-luck, although at times there may be a component of superior-merit in it as well. Thus, based on our previous discussion of success through luck, it becomes clear that, contrary to common understanding, in most cases, there is some misallocation of resources in such extreme-success, and the resulting value created for the society is not optimal in the long run.

EXTREME-SUCCESS AND CHEATING

Cheating will be discussed in fine detail in the next chapter, but to complete the discussion on extreme-success, we just need to mention the obvious: any success through cheating causes a misallocation of resources. And thus, extreme-success resulting from cheating causes the worst misallocation of resources compared to the other two mentioned above.

IN CONCLUSION

The winners whose success is based on merit under Fair Competition, are the drivers of the society's economic growth, wealth and welfare. They are the champions of the Free Market Economy. And therefore, they deserve to be wealthy and much respected in return.

However, extreme-success and extreme-wealth associated with it, is another story. As the discussion above reveals, *any sort of extreme-success contains either extreme-good-luck or cheating, and therefore creates a misallocation of* resources. Therefore, *against common understanding, cases of extreme-success are not good for the society's welfare in the long run.*

Chapter 4

CHEATING IN FREE MARKET ECONOMIES

4.1 Cheating

What Is Cheating

In a Free Market Economy, the primary principle has to be, first creating value for the society, and then, getting one's fair share of the value created.

Creating value for the society and for oneself simultaneously is the rational and ethical way, but it is also the most difficult way. Naturally, some people prefer a much easier and faster way, namely cheating.

In simple terms, therefore, *cheating is to promote one's own interests at the expense of those of the society.* And in practise, different ways of cheating are limited only by one's imagination.

Or, defining more precisely, *cheating is deliberately defying the principles of Fair Competition.* To clarify in further detail, cheating is any active or passive behaviour to prevent the establishment of Fair Competition or to dilute the principles of Fair Competition.

And to reemphasize, *cheating includes passively watching the lack of understanding and realisation of the principles of Fair Competition.* For instance, passively watching the lack of fair opportunity in the society is the cheating of the well-off (who do not need any social aid to access a good education) against the worse-off (who can not access any opportunity to education without social aid) on a grand scale.

The most common varieties of cheating occur on a micro-basis with consequences in the short to medium run. These include not competing by the rules, or having the rules made or changed to one's own benefit, or establishing all sorts of barriers to entry for potential competitors through direct or indirect means, or creating or sustaining asymmetries of information to one's own benefit, or any other creative way to decrease competition or create unfair advantage to oneself at the expense of some or all other members of the society. Although these can be recognized easily by any semi-intellectual society with a touch of social awareness, it still requires an intellectually advanced society to demand the cure through Democracy, and thus such cheating lives on happily almost in every society.

The more powerful varieties of active cheating, in the sense that they benefit the Cheaters much more than the common varieties, at the expense of decreasing the welfare of the society tremendously, occur on a macro-basis with consequences in the long run. And unfortunately, these are much more difficult to be recognized and cured by the society. These include

- preventing the establishment of fair opportunity, in education and employment for individuals, and through other means for potential competitors,
- preventing or organizing flows of goods, labour, capital, and information within and between societies such that they will protect and promote the Cheaters' interests,
- decreasing regulation to weaken the protection or the promotion of the interests of the society against those of the Cheaters,

and the most important of all,

- preventing the spread of social education to keep the social awareness of the society as low as possible as long as possible, so that cheating can go on without being detected or cured.

The Irresistible Attraction Of Power

Economics and politics are both about accumulating *power* over the others in the society. Therefore, by definition, power is a relative status, in the sense that everybody can not have it simultaneously. This simple observation reveals two major consequences.

First, power is a scarce commodity, and that it will have to be obtained through some sort of competition - preferably a fair one for the best interest of the society.

Second, again by definition, power is based on inequality, as it corresponds to some higher status relative to the others in the society. And needless to say, excessive power will require to create and keep Excessive Inequality.

The trouble with power is that, just like wealth, *the animal spirits within many people guide them not only to accumulate power, but to take it as far as possible and to keep it as long as possible.* And that is where the trouble grows: even if power is initially attained through Fair Competition, in order to be able to take it too far and to keep it for too long, eventually it will have to be used to eliminate Fair Competition, or actually any competition if possible. In short, every entity that accumulated power is bright enough to realize that *no power remains superior or eternal unless competition is eliminated. Then comes the natural urge for cheating.*

The Dilemma Of Rational Versus Ethical

Most classic economic models assume that people behave in a very rational way, but in practise the decision making process involves a delicate balance between rationality and ethics. And the one that dominates the other in case of a conflict, depends on the way the individuals believe the society will behave.

WHEN RATIONAL AND ETHICAL DIVERGES

To illustrate the process, assume somebody drops a $100 banknote while walking. The critical question here is what the next guy walking behind does when he sees the money.

One possibility is that he gives the money to the person who dropped it. This is ethical. However, is this necessarily rational?

The other possibility is that he keeps the money for himself. This is unethical. However, is this necessarily irrational?

The tricky issue here is that, what is rational depends very much on whether the guy walking behind believes that the society's action will be effected by his choice or not. This is simply because, in making his decision today, the guy walking behind will consider how the society will act in case he drops some money someday in the future, which may well be a much larger amount.

He may believe that, the society will most probably act independent of how he acts today, such that,

- the society will most probably give back his money in the future, independent of whether he gives the $100 back or not,

or,

- the society will most probably keep his money in the future, thus he will most probably not get his money back, independent of whether he gives the $100 back or not.

In both these cases, it will be ethical to give the $100 back today, but it will be rational to keep it, as it will not change his chances of getting back his money in the future. In other words, if the society is unaware of how he behaves and will act independent of his choice today, then it is unethical but rational to cheat.

Alternatively, he may believe that, the society's behaviour will be a reflection of those of its members, as everybody is well aware of how each other behaves, and therefore the society will act exactly the same way that he will act today. This means that, the society will give back his money in the future only if he gives back the $100 today, and the society will keep his money in the future if he keeps the $100 today. Therefore, in this case of total awareness, it is both ethical and rational to give back the $100 today, and it is both unethical and irrational to keep the $100 today.

WHEN RATIONAL DOMINATES THE DIVERGENCE

This simple illustration shows that, *when the society is aware of how individuals act and adjust its behaviour accordingly, ethical and rational meets*. However, when the society lacks the necessary awareness, ethical and rational diverges, and in cases where rational dominates the ethical, cheating enters the picture. Therefore, one prerequisite to opt for cheating is to assume that it will go unobserved by the society (and thus won't change the behaviour of the society), and that assumption has the highest chance to hold when the Social Intellect of the society is inadequate to understand how things work in economic and political matters.

That being said, it is also worth emphasizing that, rational can not dominate ethical at every case where they diverge. Not all of us are captives of our animal spirits.

WHEN ETHICAL DOMINATES THE DIVERGENCE

New dimensions in the study of economics, like behavioural economics and game theory developed in the recent decades, have recognized and revealed that most people base their decisions not only on rational thinking, but also on ethics and moral values.

Within the context of game theory, several studies, referred to as *games* in the jargon, have revealed the natural but neglected dimensions of human behaviour and tried to integrate them to economic analysis. One such game, known as the Ultimatum Game in the jargon (which was discussed in Section 2.2) reveals that an individual will choose to be fair when he knows that others may react strongly, and even irrationally, if they become aware that they are treated unfairly. But even beyond the fear of others' reaction, people mostly choose to be fair mainly to satisfy their own conscience, at least when the cost of being ethical is not too high or they do not have a valid excuse to behave differently. One game that reveals such preference is known as the Dictator Game in the jargon[15], where somebody with the sole authority to make a choice, has to choose between two options that allocate some benefits between himself and some other person. In the first option he will get 10 units of benefit to himself and 2 units to the other person, and in the second option he will get 9 units of benefit to himself and 5 units to the other person. In a pure rationalistic approach, he is expected to choose the first option as it maximises his own benefit. But in practise, many people choose the second option, as a little sacrifice from their own benefit will bring a significant improvement on the benefit of the other person[16].

In short, most people would actually prefer to integrate ethics and moral values in their decision making process, especially when they believe that others in the society is behaving in the same way too.

WHEN ECONOMIC HARDSHIP DOMINATES ETHICS

The balancing of rational versus ethical in the decision making process is another example of complicated relations in human behaviour. Just like in many other cases, the effects of each on the outcome seems to be non-linear. In simple terms, when one faces a matter of survival, including economic hardship, rationality talks louder than ethics and naturally dictates the priority of self interest over other issues. When one is struggling to survive, ethics and values unfortunately become items of luxury. For that reason, effects of ethics may remain lower in under-developed economies, unless there are other strong cultural norms that support ethical behaviour. By the same token, as the economic and intellectual development of a society rises, ethics and moral values get the chance to speak louder and balance out rationality in decision making.

Who Cheats

As the ways to cheat are infinite in practise, so are the types of Cheaters. But some cases are more common than others.

The first type that comes to mind are those who lack the merit (primarily the discipline and the hard work) to win under Fair Competition. They may choose to cheat, naively believing that they can win through cheating. Unfortunately, in most cases where one can cheat, others can and will cheat too. Consequently, there will soon arise new conditions where all Cheaters will now have to compete against each other again, but this time with different rules that may span from unethical all the way to illegal. But again, winning through such competition will necessitate some different sort of merit based on different abilities, and thus the end result may not change for most.

The second and the most dangerous type are those who are greedy. They choose to cheat not because they are not winning under Fair Competition, but because they are not satisfied with their decent success under Fair Competition. The trouble for the society here is that, these are already successful competitors who are in search of further success, but this time at the expense of the society. And if they succeed further by cheating, they will accumulate more power in time, and eventually may create some concentrated power within their market, also known as a monopoly. And as will be discussed in the next chapter, monopolies are nightmares for the society.

The third type are those who are forced to cheat, as all their rivals are cheating in their market and thus it became impossible to stay competitive and survive on merit alone.

The fourth, and the most interesting of all, is where the merited competitors cheat not because of greed but because of their fear of the intervention of luck.

Why Even The Merited Winners May Become Cheaters

THE FEAR OF INTERVENTION OF LUCK

The alternate paths to success are, by definition, also the paths to power.

In principle, if success and power are attained through merit, they can be kept at decent levels in the long run.

In practise, however, even in cases of decent success, there are many occasions where the source of success is, or considered to be, a blend of merit and luck - where luck is an uncontrollable variable. And even in the cases where the winners owe their success primarily to merit, rather than a balanced blend, they may still suspect that,

- they might have had good luck on their side, or at least have not faced an unlucky event when they won in this round, however in the next round, their luck may reverse: they may not have any good luck, or worse, they may face bad luck,

or,

- they might have won because some of their rivals have faced bad luck in this round, and in the next round these rivals will not face such bad luck again, or worse, may have good luck on their side.

In short, unless a winner-on-merit believes that his superiority in merit is strong enough to overcome any potential changes in luck, he may be inclined to cheat in order to sustain his success.

Such tendency will naturally be stronger in cases where the margin of success is small relative to potential effects of luck. And in the extremely competitive environments of our time, it is difficult to have high margins of success based on merit alone, unless one is extremely merited (and extreme merit necessitates extreme intellect on top of education, experience and hard work). Therefore, in times like ours, many moderately merited winners may be inclined to cheat at least a little once in a while.

THE SENSE OF INJUSTICE IN SOCIETIES WITH WEAK SOCIAL INTELLECT

The situation is worse in societies with inadequate Social Intellect, where cheating is widespread. Under such conditions, on the one hand, the winners-on-merit may think that in case they had cheated their success would have been much bigger and stronger. And on the other hand, the society, being weak on Social Intellect, pours fuel to the fire by respecting the Cheaters way more than the winners-on-merit, based on the Cheaters' bigger success, without considering the path taken to achieve that success. Then, the animal spirits within the winners-on-merit, however deep down they could have been buried, will rise to shout for justice – but this time for one to be attained through the wrong path, namely cheating. And this time, at least for some, feelings of injustice may dominate ethics.

THE DESIRE FOR EXTREME-SUCCESS

It goes without saying that, when there is a desire to reach extreme-success, the tendency to cheat may be very strong.

And worse, as discussed by the end of Chapter 3, even in cases where extreme-success initially came as a blend of extreme-merit and extreme-luck, the desire to sustain it will call for cheating, as in an environment of Fair Competition extreme-success may not survive for too long.

Targets Of Cheating

In choosing their victims to cheat on, the Cheaters have no boundaries apart from their imagination and they usually enjoy the luxury of cheating against many targets simultaneously to maximise their own interests. Still, some common targets can be classified.

The first target is their rival competitors. In general, once themselves are in, Cheaters try to create high barriers to entry so that new competitors can not join the market to increase competition. And to cheat against the existing ones, they usually try to effect the rule making to their benefit, or at least make sure that the existing rules will not be enforced upon them while they are enforced on their rivals – as will be discussed in Chapter 6. The bottom line is always the same: to consolidate as much power as possible within the market and thus minimise competition, at the expense of not only their rivals, but their customers, suppliers and the society.

The second target is their counter parties, namely their customers and suppliers – including the labour they utilize in production of goods or services. One way of cheating against all counter parties is to have a dominant status within the market and dictating its own conditions to others - as will be discussed in Chapter 5. Another common way with customers is utilizing the naturally existing asymmetries of information between all producers and customers, to their own benefit – as will be discussed in the next section.

The third target, the biggest and the easiest of all, is the society. As discussed in Chapter 2, creating and benefitting from externalities, at the expense of the society, is a common way. But an easier and more fruitful approach is to cheat against the state, which actually is equivalent to indirectly cheating against the society in major proportions, as the state is financed by the taxes paid by the society. Doing business with state institutions under unfair conditions attained in many ways, from utilising asymmetries of information all the way to benefitting from corruption is a well known practise in almost all societies. And the lower the Social Intellect of the society, the wider the spread of cheating against the state, and thus the higher the damage the society endures because of cheating.

Tools of Cheating

The tools of cheating, in practise, are only limited by the Cheaters' imagination. In principle, however, two tools are the basis for almost all others. And the following discussion will therefore focus on these two primary tools, namely, *asymmetries of information* and *corruption of agents*.

4.2 Cheating Utilising Asymmetry of Information

Cheating Against Customers

ASYMMETRY OF INFORMATION

Asymmetry of information refers to the case where the participants on the supply and demand sides have different levels of information on the issues relevant to a transaction.

In principle, Fair Competition requires all relevant information to be available to all participants in every market. Unfortunately, this is almost never the case in practise, and *asymmetries of information exist as an integral part of any market where supply meets demand for any product or service, in both economics and politics. This makes asymmetry of information an inherent weakness of both the economic and political systems – a weakness that is widely utilised by the Cheaters.*

HOW CHEATING BASED ON ASYMMETRY OF INFORMATION
EMERGES AND SPREADS

To understand what happens when some information asymmetry exists, consider a market where there is perfect competition between the suppliers (no barriers, no price setting power etc.), however, the customers can only appreciate the differences in some attributes of the product but are unable to observe the differences in some other attributes, as it happens with most of the products of our time. In such cases, competition naturally works only on the attributes of the product that are observable by the customers. Consequently, it is convenient to cheat on the attributes that the customers can not observe.

To illustrate, assume that the customers can observe the colour and size of a product, but not the chemicals or the materials it is made of. Then, as competition gets fierce, some of the producers will start to cheat and use the cheapest quality chemicals with the lowest cost, even though these chemicals may harm the customers in the long run. This way, these Cheaters will be able to decrease their prices and gain competitive edge while still staying profitable. Once this dynamic starts, the rest of the producers face two options. They may reject to use those harmful materials and as a result can not decrease their prices, and become uncompetitive and leave the market. Or, if they want to survive in the market, they will have to start cheating too, and utilize the same materials to be able to decrease their costs and therefore their prices to competitive levels. Therefore, *once a competitor starts to use the advantage of the asymmetry of information to its own benefit at the expense of the society, all others have to follow suit in order to stay competitive.* In our case, all the surviving producers end up using those low-quality cheap chemicals in their products, collectively cheating against the customers.

The unfortunate but significant observation here is that, *even in competitive markets, any attribute of any product that goes unobserved by the consumers will be subject to cheating. The reflection of this vital observation to macro-economic and political matters, and its consequences, are of paramount importance,* as will be discussed in the coming chapters and books.

ASYMMETRY OF INFORMATION GETS WORSE AS THE COMPLEXITY OF THE ENVIRONMENT RISES

In the simple environment of the good old days in the distant past, the information asymmetries between the participants in any market used to be much less than they are today, keeping their negative effects limited on the society. But in today's environment which gets ever more complex every passing day, consumers need to make a million decisions on a million complex issues continuously, from economics to politics, and in aggregate they need a huge amount of information to make rational decisions on every issue. Naturally, most members of the society are incapable of accessing and processing that much information, and have to consent to making decisions based on inadequate information presented to them in all economic and political matters. And that creates ever growing opportunities for the Cheaters.

CHEATERS DELIBERATELY CREATE ASYMMETRIES OF INFORMATION

Cheating utilising asymmetries of information can work in different ways. In the simplest case, the Cheaters deliberately present only some portion of the whole set of facts that have to be known by the customers to enable a rational decision, and then they cheat on the hidden portion.

In more advanced cases, the Cheaters present some portion of the story, such that it is true, but will most probably be misunderstood by the customers, and will result in their acting to the benefit of the Cheaters rather than of their own. For instance, an expensive product may be presented to increase the customers' life span when used continuously, and that may actually be true, however, the fact that was conveniently forgotten to be mentioned is that the expected increase is just a couple of weeks.

And in cases where the customers fail to misunderstand the presented portion by themselves, the Cheaters help them to do so, through creating a misperception of the facts.

PERCEPTION MANAGEMENT

Sometimes a producer develops some competitive advantage over his rivals in some attribute of a product, but unfortunately that attribute is not critical enough to increase the value of the product for the customers. In such cases, the supplier deliberately creates a misperception through a marketing campaign, arguing that the attribute that he managed to improve is actually a very critical one for the value of the product but the customers just fail to recognize it. If the campaign succeeds, it creates a different sort of asymmetry of information, where, that particular attribute which the supplier knows to be unimportant, is promoted to be an important one in the eyes of the consumers, guiding them to think that the promoter's product is more valuable than those of his rivals. As the demand shifts to that product for no real reason apart from the creation of a misperception by the Cheater, it will actually cause a misallocation of resources within the economy, harming both the consumers and the society. And just as perception management can be used to over-promote a positive attribute of one's own product, it can also be used to over-promote a negative attribute of a competitor's product.

The use of perception management to cheat against both the rival competitors and the customers is one of the most common approaches in economics. And worse, it is also a very powerful tool to cheat in politics (where the customers are the voters) with significant consequences for the society in the long run – as will be discussed in the coming chapters.

REGULATION AND CHEATING ON INFORMATION ASYMMETRY

In the complex environment of our day, on the one hand, consumers lack the time and ability to access and process all the information required for making rational decisions on the infinitely many economic choices they face, and on the other hand, many Cheaters try to utilise this asymmetry of information to promote their own interests against those of the consumers. The only way out is the appropriate regulation of the markets such that the interests of the consumers (and thus of the society) are protected as much as possible.

Regulation, therefore, is of critical importance in preventing the cheating against the consumers and the society, through utilising asymmetries of information. Unfortunately, *societies almost never appreciate the significance of regulation, while the Cheaters almost always do* – both for a solid reason.

Concentrated Benefits Distributed Costs

It is easy to see that cheating creates a benefit to the Cheater at the expense of his customers. What is not so easy to see but actually more important is that, as will be explained in Section 4.4, *the total harm inflicted on the customers is much bigger than the total benefit of the Cheater.* Therefore, if the harm is inflicted only on a small number of customers, the reaction of these customers will naturally be stronger than the effort of the Cheater, making cheating very difficult or even impossible. However, when the benefit is concentrated and therefore is important for the Cheater, while the harm is distributed to very many customers such that it does not even get noticed by any of them, cheating suddenly becomes much easier. Therefore, *the precondition for effective and sustainable cheating is the asymmetry that there is a concentrated benefit on the Cheater's side while the cost is distributed to many customers.*

This phenomenon, which we may call *Concentrated Benefits versus Distributed Costs* is the essence of cheating on customers through information asymmetry. And exactly for that reason -as will be discussed in Section 4.3-, *cheating against the state is so attractive: costs are distributed so widely and indirectly to the society that nobody notices their existence and thus no opposition materializes.*

THE CATASTROPHIC TREND

Thanks to the technological advancements of the latest decades, every passing day many markets integrate further and expand, even into global proportions, usually without increasing competition but rather increasing the concentration on the production side. This practically means a further concentration of benefits on the production (supply) side, while a wider distribution of costs on the customer (demand) side, skyrocketing the efficiency of the Concentrated Benefits versus Distributed Costs phenomenon. Consequently, both the potential benefits of cheating for the producers and the harm to be inflicted on the customers (and indirectly on the societies as there are misallocations of resources) are exponentially increasing, fuelling further cheating[17]. And, as discussed in Book One, the weakening of the Social Intellect of the societies is everywhere to guard this trend.

REGULATION IS THE KEY, REGULATORS ARE THE TARGET

Cases of concentrated benefits versus distributed costs, therefore, introduce a struggle between the Cheaters versus the customers and the society. On the one hand, proper regulation comes out to be the key to protect and promote the interests of the customers and the society. On the other hand, the Cheaters, being the concentrated interest groups in their sectors or markets, target the Regulators to direct them to mis-regulate, such that the interests of the Cheaters will be promoted against those of the rest.

And targeting the Regulators consists of two basic ways. One is misguiding the Regulators utilising the asymmetries of information between the Cheaters and the Regulators, as will be discussed next. The other is going a step further and trying to corrupt the Regulators utilising any potential weaknesses in their ethical values, as will be discussed in the following section.

Misguiding Regulators, To Cheat Against All Targets

The previous analysis on asymmetry of information in this section has focused on cheating against the customers. But when the Regulators are the target of cheating based on asymmetry of information, all potential victims take their share.

In some cases, the direct victims (customers, suppliers, labour, or rival competitors) do not have the power to counter balance the misguidance, and the society, as the indirect victim, fails to see the harm that comes its way because of the inadequacy of its Social Intellect. In other cases, the society is the direct victim, but it has diluted interests on an individual basis and thus still fails to counter react through political means. For these reasons, lobbying on Regulators and misguiding them to regulate to the benefit of the Cheaters at the expense of the rest, is one of the most preferred ways of cheating.

To prevent cheating through the process of lobbying to misguide the Regulators, the information asymmetry between the Cheaters and the Regulators should be minimised. And contrary to the case with individual customers where the prevention of asymmetry of information is practically impossible, *the prevention of the asymmetry of information between the Cheaters and the Regulators is possible – in case the society is intellectual enough to demand it politically*. We will discuss this in Chapter 6.

4.3 Agency Relation And Corruption

The Agency Relation

Everyday, individuals have to deal with a large number of issues and make decisions on them, and as handling all these decisions by themselves is a practical impossibility, they need to utilise agents who will act on their behalf. This practical necessity creates *principal - agent relations.* The best known case for agency relation is the one between the shareholders (as the principal) and the managers (as the agent) in a corporate environment. But the more important case is the agency relation between the society (as the principal) and the Politicians, the Regulators and the State Bureaucrats (as the direct or indirect agents) in a Democracy.

When a principal delegates the duty of acting on his behalf to an agent, one primary assumption behind that delegation is that the ability of the agent in dealing with that specific issue is much superior to that of the principal. And a second primary assumption, which is even more significant, but much weaker, is that the agent has the perfect goodwill to act on the best interest of the principal independent of the agent's own interest. Unfortunately, most of the times the best interest of the agent is not the same as the best interest of the principal, and this *conflict of interests* may change the behaviour of the agent, such that the agent acts to promote its own interest at the expense of that of the principal, and creates an *agency problem.*

On the agent's side, this cheating behaviour arises especially when the principal is considered to be too naïve to be aware of such cheating.

As discussed in detail in Book One of this series, when the complexity of the world rises, both the asymmetry of expertise and the asymmetry of information between the agent and the principal also rise, to the disadvantage of the principal. This will significantly decrease the ability of the principal to detect any cheating on the agent's side. As a consequence, the amount of cheating the agent may get away with - without being detected by the principal- increases, which in turn increases the potential benefits the agent can get for himself at the expense of the principal. And this further motivates the agent to cheat on the principal.

The trouble gets worse when macro-economic and political fronts are considered, simply because the society, as the principal, may at best observe the macro-decisions made by the Politicians, but is too distant to the micro-decisions made by the rest of the political agents within the state and bureaucracy. Thus, in the complex world of our day, where the Social Intellect of the society is weaker than it used to be, it is easier for these political agents to act against the best interest of the society and get away with that.

Corruption

Cheating is a one-sided activity. The Cheater acts alone against its rival competitors, consumers, suppliers, Regulators, and the society, to maximise his own interest at their expense.

In contrast, corruption is two-sided. A Cheater on one side, and a corrupt agent on the other side, cooperating to promote their own interests at the expense of the principal of the corrupt agent. In other words, the corrupt agent is cheating against his principal, in cooperation with the Cheater, to share the benefits reaped from his principal between himself and the Cheater.

In general, this is a micro-operation where the deal is between the Cheater and the corrupt agent, and thus not known by the victim, namely the principal. Therefore, there is no asymmetry of information between the Cheater and the corrupt agent, but there is a terrible asymmetry of information between the corrupt agent and his principal.

Many sample cases of corruption will be examined in the following sub-section, but before proceeding further, clarifying some significant issues is necessary.

In many cases, corruption involves the participation of some political agent. In such cases, the Cheater is an economic actor, trying to promote his own economic benefit with the help of a corrupt political agent. If the

Cheater has some sort of economic deal with the state, then the society, as the main principal, is the direct victim of corruption. However, even in cases where the Cheater is just trying to promote his economic interest at the expense of other private victims (customers, rivals etc.) with the help of a corrupt Regulator through deliberate mis-regulation, still the society will be an indirect victim, simply because any sort of corruption will cause a misallocation of resources that damages the interest of the society in the long run.

In other cases, a Cheater may just be trying to promote his economic interest at the expense of other private victims (customers, suppliers, rivals etc.), this time with the help of the target victim's corrupted agents (thus, without the involvement of any political agent). Still, the society will still be an indirect victim in the long run because of the misallocation of resources resulting from such cheating and corruption.

Finally, it also possible that two corrupt agents, each acting on behalf of different principals, may cooperate to promote their own benefits against those of their principals simultaneously. Once again, in addition to the two principals being the direct victims, the society will be an indirect victim as the harm from the resulting misallocation of resources will be felt in the long run.

In short, *any type of cheating and corruption involving any potential cooperators acting against the interests of any victim will eventually harm the society, and thus requires the close attention of the society.*

Cheating In Cooperation With Corrupted Agents

CHEATING AGAINST THE STATE UTILISING CORRUPTED POLITICAL AGENTS

In cases where the Cheater is an economic actor trying to promote his own interest in his dealings with the state, at the expense of the society as the direct victim, he needs a corruptible political agent or a bureaucrat within the state.

Such cheating with the cooperation of a corrupt agent can be done in many ways, including but not limited to the classic ones below:

- If the Cheater is involved as a counter-party in the common commercial operations of the state, a corrupt agent will help in both directions. When the Cheater is on the supply side, the corrupt agent will let the state buy his products or services at above market prices. And when the Cheater is on the demand side, the corrupt agent will let the state sell its products at below market prices.

- If the Cheater wants to be involved in the investment projects of the state, as a potential seller of some service, the corrupt agent may direct an auction unfairly to the Cheater, sometimes with extremely favourable profit margins or conditions.

- If the Cheater wants to be involved in the privatisations of state owned companies, or the sale of some state property or land, as a potential buyer, the corrupt agent may direct an auction to the Cheater, usually at lower than fair prices, leaving a potential high profit to the Cheater at the expense of the state.

- If the Cheater will be involved in the financing of the state, as a potential lender, the corrupt agent may make the state borrow at higher than necessary interest rates, increasing the profit margin of the Cheater. Alternatively, if the Cheater will need financing by the state, the corrupt agent may direct some state funds to the Cheater, usually at lower than market rates, and sometimes for excessively risky projects.

By the nature of the process, in all such cases, the higher the value of the deal arranged by the corrupt agent for the Cheater, the higher needs to be the rank of the corrupted agent within the state hierarchy, and the higher the benefit to be transferred to the corrupt agent.

CHEATING AGAINST CUSTOMERS, SUPPLIERS AND RIVAL COMPETITORS UTILISING CORRUPTED REGULATORS

In Section 4.2, the case with mis-regulation through the misguidance of Regulators was discussed. Whenever such misguidance does not work, similar results can be achieved by the Cheaters through cooperation with corrupted Regulators who will mis-regulate deliberately, with similar direct consequences for customers, suppliers and rival competitors. And even if such deliberate mis-regulation may stay at micro-levels on a case by case basis, all such micro-level cases will eventually get aggregated and indirectly harm the society at macro proportions in the long run.

CHEATING AGAINST CUSTOMERS, SUPPLIERS AND RIVAL COMPETITORS UTILISING THEIR CORRUPTED AGENTS

It is also possible to find corruptible agents in private companies that have some commercial relation with the Cheater. And then, just like cooperating with corrupted state agents, Cheaters can easily cooperate with corrupted agents of their customers, suppliers or rival competitors. This way, they can sell at higher prices to customers or buy at lower prices from suppliers, they can finance risky projects or access cheap financing, they can get insider information from their rivals or transfer know-how to get unfair advantage in competition, etc. Once again, such micro-level harms resulting from cheating and corruption among private parties, will still get aggregated and indirectly harm the society at macro proportions in the long run.

4.4   Fallacy Of Cheating

Cheating Is Not A Zero-Sum Game

Fair Competition results in the optimal allocation of resources within an economy and maximises the wealth of the society. Consequently, *cheating, being the destroyer of Fair Competition, causes a misallocation of resources that significantly decreases the total wealth of the society.*

Conceptually, the society is the sum of the Cheater plus the rest of the society. In this simple equation, on the one hand, cheating decreases the total wealth of the society, and on the other hand, increases the personal wealth of the Cheater. It directly follows that, the magnitude of decrease in the wealth of the rest of the society is much larger than the magnitude of increase in the wealth of the Cheater. Therefore, *cheating is not a zero-sum game where the benefit of the Cheater equals to the loss of the rest of the society, but a destroyer of the total wealth of the society such that the loss of the rest of the society is much larger than the benefit of the Cheater.*

In other words, the Cheater will get a relatively small benefit in return for a high expense for the rest of the society, as the total wealth of the Cheater plus the rest of the society will fall due to cheating[18]. This observation reveals strong consequences that usually go unrealized, even by the Cheaters.

Cheating And The Competitors' Dilemma

Competition is at the heart of economics, where each competitor faces a decision on the way he competes against all others. He can compete fairly or he can cheat. This critical decision, that was partially discussed in Section 4.1, deserves a closer analysis.

The situation comes out to be a classical dilemma well known in the game theory, that just needs an adjustment to our case. In the table below, the rows and columns show how an individual competitor and the society may choose to behave, and the values in the cells show the potential benefit (or, harm if the value is negative) they will face accordingly.

	SOCIETY CHEATS	SOCIETY DOES NOT CHEAT
INDIVIDUAL CHEATS	society : -40 individual : (-40)+(+15) = **-25**	society : +30 individual : (+30)+(+15) = **+45**
INDIVIDUAL DOES NOT CHEAT	society : -40 individual : (-40)+(+5) = **-35**	society : +30 individual : (+30)+(+5) = **+35**

In the table, it is assumed that, when an individual competitor competes fairly, his benefit from his own economic activity is (+5), but when he cheats his benefit will rise to (+15). And when (the rest of) the society competes fairly, an almost-optimal allocation of resources creates a value of (+30) for all the members of the society, while when (the rest of) the society cheats all together, the misallocation of resources will create a major loss of (-40) for all the members of the society. The net benefit an individual will get, is the sum of his benefit from his own economic activity based on his own decision, plus the benefit he incurs as a result of the society's decision.

It is clear from the table that the best case for an individual (with +45 overall benefit) is when he cheats but the rest of the society plays fair. Thus *every Cheater prefers the case where only he can cheat, but not the rest of the society*.

It is also clear from the table that *the nightmare case for an individual competitor* (with -35 overall loss) *is when he plays fair but the rest of the society cheats*.

The other two cases seem to be trivial. If both the individual competitor and the society cheats, all will end up losing (-25). If neither the individual competitor nor the society cheats they will all end up benefitting (+35).

The crucial observation is what will happen in practise. To see that, consider the cases from the individual competitor's perspective.

It is already clear that, when the society does not cheat, it is for the best interest of an individual competitor to cheat, as that will enable to rise his benefit from (+35) to (+45). And it also clear that, when the society cheats, it is better for the individual competitor to cheat, as that will decrease his loss from (-35) to (-25). And this gives a net conclusion for each individual competitor: each of them should cheat independent of what the society does.

The unfortunate end result is that, when all individual competitors cheat, then by definition, the society cheats, and all will end up at a net loss of (-25). This is exactly why *in any unregulated (or mis-regulated) environment where cheating can not be prevented, everybody will have to cheat and they all will have to bear the very negative result of that society-wide behaviour.*

To escape this trap, it is necessary for the society to have adequate Social Intellect such that it will demand and get the establishment of Fair Competition through democratic means, and have cheating prevented through appropriate regulation. And when all competitors have no choice but to play fairly, only then the society will end up at the case where nobody cheats - and all individuals will benefit (+35) in the illustration above.

From another perspective, *having adequate Social Intellect will enable all the competitors in the society, and thus the society itself, to realise that, their real choice is between the cases where either everybody cheats or nobody cheats.*

When some competitors greedily shoot for increasing their benefits [to (+45) in the illustration] *and start to cheat, nobody wants to stay behind to experience a nightmare* [the loss of (-35) in the illustration] *and thus everybody starts to cheat, and the society eventually ends up at the bad choice* [where everybody loses (-25) in the illustration].

The only way to reach the good choice [where everybody wins (+35) in the illustration] *is the prevention of cheating for every competitor, through the solid political demand of the society that eventually forces the Regulators to have and to enforce proper regulation.*

Trapped In The Fallacy

The analysis above revealed that the best case for an individual is when he cheats but the rest of the society plays fair. But the same analysis also revealed that when one competitor starts to cheat, the rest have no choice but to cheat as well, ending up at the worst case for everyone. And unfortunately, this worst case is the common practice in all societies with inadequate Social Intellect.

One interesting question is, in the worst case that is common in practise, how come the individual competitors who cheat believe that they live in a world where only they can cheat but not the others.

The unfortunate answer stems from the observation made in Section 4.2: in most cases of cheating, the benefit of his own cheating in his own market is concentrated and thus can easily be observed by the Cheater, while the costs arising from the cheating of other Cheaters in other markets are distributed and thus mostly escape the attention of the Cheater.

Every individual in a society is some sort of a supplier in his own market, while he is a consumer in many other markets. Every Cheater recognizes the explicit extra benefit he gets from cheating in the market where he is on the supply side, but fails to observe that he is actually losing much more than that implicitly in the aggregate of all the other markets where he is on the demand side. *The concentrated benefits versus distributed costs phenomenon fools the Cheater this time, as his gain from cheating is concentrated in the market in which he is on the supply side, while the individually-minor-but-in-the-aggregate-major-losses he experiences are distributed to the very many markets where he is on the demand side and thus escape his attention.*

In our illustration above, the Cheater recognizes that by cheating he increases his personal benefit from (+5) to (+15), however, he fails to see that when he cheats others will cheat too, and that will introduce an aggregate major loss of (-40) on himself, ruining his overall wealth and making him end up at (-25) in total. Thus, the lack of economic awareness of this two-sided dynamic plays a significant role in spreading cheating in the economy.

THE DEPTH OF THE TRAP

Assume that a competitor in a market somehow became aware of the concentrated benefits versus distributed costs phenomenon, and realised that when he cheats others will cheat too and consequently they all will face a huge net loss. Unfortunately, such realisation will not suffice for him to cease cheating. As revealed by the illustration above, the worst case for an individual is when he plays fair but others cheat. Therefore, if he knows that most of the rest of the society lacks such awareness and thus continue to cheat, he will not cease to cheat either.

The bottom line is that, the awareness of the concentrated benefits versus distributed costs phenomenon will help to increase the tendency of all competitors to play fair, however, they will not actually start to play fair unless they are sure that others will play fair too. And the only way to ensure this is through proper regulation and flawless enforcement.

A MATTER OF SOCIAL INTELLECT, AGAIN

In a society with adequate Social Intellect, the awareness of the concentrated benefits versus distributed costs phenomenon would be widespread, and consequently the political demand for the establishment of Fair Competition would be strong. The resulting enaction and enforcement of proper regulations all throughout the economy would then make sure that nobody will be able to cheat in any market.

Unfortunately, the reverse is also true. *Cheating is a consequence of inadequate Social Intellect and the resulting lack of political demand for Fair Competition, and thus inevitably becomes an economy-wide phenomenon: it spreads very fast to all the markets unless it is prevented in each and every market.*

4.5   Cheating And The Society

Cheating And Fairness

In the previous sections, the negative effects of cheating on the wealth of the society are analysed, and it is clarified that it will be wise for the society to promote Fair Competition against cheating to maximise its overall wealth.

The effects of cheating are also strongly felt on another social dimension, namely on the moral values of the society. The society would like to see that the competitors who deserve to win eventually win, and those who deserve to lose eventually lose. In other words, the Fair Players who compete on merit should succeed, and the Cheaters should fail. But when there is wide spread cheating, many of those who deserve to fail eventually win, and to make matters worse, many of those who deserve to succeed eventually lose. This undesired outcome hurts the sense of fairness of the society, and more importantly, of the Fair Players.

CHEATERS HIDING BEHIND FAIR PLAYERS

In most societies and markets, there are still both Fair Players and Cheaters, as some competitors prioritise ethical values over further increasing their benefits through cheating. The danger is that, the Cheaters' winning through an unfair competition in many cases, hurts the feelings of the society, and thus a strong reaction may emerge in time unless these feelings are taken care of. For that reason, a primary strategy pursued by the Cheaters is to behave like, and therefore to hide behind, the Fair Players who succeed on merit. In societies with inadequate Social Intellect where what one says counts more than what one actually does, this strategy works effectively. As a matter of comedy, or tragedy, *it is common to see the Cheaters defend the value of fairness with the loudest voices around.* Their basic purpose is to make the society believe that the system is actually fair and therefore has to be preserved as it is – together with the Cheaters in it. If the society takes this bait and fails to improve its economic and political systems to establish Fair Competition and eliminate the Cheaters, it pays the price in the long run.

THE FOOLISHNESS OF THE UNDESERVED LOSERS

In a society where cheating becomes a common path to success, many people who try to compete on merit will become losers in an undeserved way. Their natural reaction is supposed to be a demand for Fair Competition which will eliminate the Cheaters from the system. However, most of those undeserved losers, who may be hard working labour or capable professionals, but just lack the Social Intellect to see what is really going wrong, and thus buy the picture painted by the Cheaters, end up believing that the winners in the current system are the deserved ones within the rules of the current system. Such logic immediately drives them to think that something is terribly wrong with the system itself, rather than with the competitors. For that reason, *whenever inequality rises to unacceptable levels as result of widespread cheating, many people tend to support the populists advertising to change the system* to introduce more equality, *rather than supporting the rational politicians who will preserve the system but just eliminate cheating* to decrease such excessive inequality towards acceptable levels. And as history has demonstrated over and over again, when the society follows the wrong leaders, it can not find the right path and pays the price in the long run.

THE MISERY OF THE DECENT WINNERS

Another tragic case is that of the Fair Players in markets with widespread cheating, who managed to have some decent success based on their merit, but not as much as they would have if they had cheated. As if their own emotional reaction against facing such unfairness is not enough, *when the society fails to differentiate the Cheaters from the Fair Players and respect the Cheaters more than the Fair Players, the Fair Players start to question the rationality of their choice. And that is when cheating starts to spread much faster in the society.*

Fairness And Wisdom

As analysed throughout this chapter, cheating creates a misallocation of resources and therefore decreases the wealth of the society in the long run. Moreover, cheating naturally creates a strong sense of unfairness in the society, as the society would like to see those who fairly compete on merit to win, rather than the Cheaters. And once cheating starts, it spreads fast and wide, and eventually the whole society loses materially and morally – including the Cheaters.

Therefore, *establishing Fair Competition is not only a matter of ethics, but also a matter of rationality for the society.*

Consequently, in a society with adequate Social Intellect, *the establishment of Fair Competition and the prevention of cheating can not be left to the mercy of the ethical values, but must be properly handled by appropriate lawmaking and enforcement –* as will be discussed in Chapter 6.

Chapter 5

COMPETITION AT THE EXTREMES

5.1   Competition And The Optimal Dose

Competition is at the heart of the free markets. In principle, it encourages the supply side to do its best and enables the demand side to get the best. In practice, however, life is not that simple. Just like anything else that is good, competition works best when it exists at an optimal dose. Unfortunately, it has a strong tendency to move towards the extremes and heavily harm many market participants on both the supply and the demand sides.

One extreme, the case of under-competition, and the troubles associated with it, are relatively well recognised in principle, but mostly left uncured in practise, especially during the latest decades.

The other extreme, the case of over-competition, and the troubles associated with it, are little recognised, and let alone being cured, are actually fuelled by the policies of the state institutions.

And the worst of all, the creation of over-competition in some markets as a result of the emergence of under-competition in others, is not recognised at all, and continues to spread and inflict an ever-rising harm to the overall economy.

5.2   Concentration Of Power, Monopolies And Under-competition

Concentration Of Power

In a free market, once a company catches a significant competitive advantage, it starts to accumulate power against its rivals. In many cases such accumulation will result in some concentration of power, but only temporarily, as its rivals will catch up and nullify its advantage first, and dilute its concentration of power next. However, if the company somehow manages to sustain its competitive advantage and build on it for long enough, it will pass a critical mass in either market share and/or technological advancement and/or efficiency and/or financial strength, beyond which its concentration of power will become too difficult to overcome. And then only one more step, namely cheating, is left to make its concentration of power permanent – virtually eliminating the competition in the market. And the urge to keep power makes it too difficult to resist taking that step.

FAIR COMPETITION VERSUS CONCENTRATION OF POWER

Fair Competition, the only way to maximise the wealth of a society in the long run, is by definition *fair* plus *competition*. It follows that, if there is *cheating* and/or *a permanent concentration of power* in a market, then Fair Competition has ceased to exist in that market.

CREATING CONCENTRATION OF POWER THROUGH CHEATING

As discussed in the previous chapter, when one competitor starts to cheat, the others will have to follow suit sooner or later. But if many competitors can cheat equally well (at the expense of the customer or the society), although fairness is lost in the market, competition may still survive and a concentration of power may never emerge. In this case, the overall wealth of the society still decreases due to the loss of fairness in competition, but the damage is somewhat limited as competition has survived.

But in cases where one Cheater is better at the art of cheating than the others, not only fairness but also competition will eventually be lost. The competitive advantage obtained through cheating then creates a permanent concentration of power. In this case where competition itself is weakened or has totally disappeared, the wealth of the society will decrease way beyond the level caused by the loss of fairness alone. Therefore, *the emergence of some permanent concentration of power and the loss of competition, is even worse than the loss of fairness*.

CREATING CONCENTRATION OF POWER WITHOUT CHEATING

Concentration of power does not necessarily arise out of cheating. By the nature of free markets, just through a competitor's merit and/or luck, some competitive advantage may emerge and in turn create some concentration of power.

For instance, a competitor may gain an advantage through launching an innovative product or service, or developing a new commercial idea. If the innovation is significant enough, the competitor may enjoy the power of creative destruction that can enable him to attain some concentration of power within its market.

Such emergence of a concentration of power may weaken competition in the market temporarily, but if fairness survives in the market, the other competitors will eventually catch up and restore competition. Such occurrences of temporary concentrations of power will not decrease the wealth of the society, but just on the contrary will increase it in the long run. This is simply because, the temporary high profits enjoyed during the concentrated-power period will motivate all competitors to be innovative and reap similar benefits once in a while.

The trouble starts if a competitor that attained some concentration of power does not want to give it up and revert to cheating to destroy both fairness and competition permanently. If it succeeds, and unfortunately it has a high chance of success as it starts cheating from the very advantageous position of having a concentrated power in the market, then a temporary concentration created within an environment of Fair

Competition will turn into a permanent one that deliberately destroys Fair Competition and harms the society.

AVOIDING LOSS OF FAIR COMPETITION

A permanent concentration of power, therefore, can emerge in two different sequences. Either by losing fairness through cheating first, many times followed by a loss of competition in the later stages, or, by losing competition first, followed by losing fairness in later stages.

Both practically mean that, in order to sustain Fair Competition in every market, a society must protect both fairness and competition delicately, through demanding the creation and enforcement of proper regulations, which can only be possible by increasing the awareness of its members through rising their Social Intellect.

Monopolies And Oligopolies

If a competitor attains too much concentration of power and manages to keep it for too long, it will eventually wipe out any serious competition and practically become a *monopoly* in its market. Notice that, the emergence of a monopoly does not necessitate the elimination of all competition, but just the over-weakening of it, such that the competitor in the monopoly position can become the sole price and/or condition setter in the market.

In the classic case, the monopoly becomes the price setter for the product of the market, rather than being a price taker, and this is considered to be the primary symptom of a monopoly position which in turn alerts the Regulators for counter action. In the cases of the recent decades, however, the prices of some products or services ceased to be explicitly stated in monetary terms, but rather are charged in hidden ways in terms of acquired personal information of the customer, under the unilateral conditions set by the suppliers of the products or services. For that reason, *the Regulators failed to recognise and act in time against the developing concentration of power on the markets based on information and communication technologies*, and eventually faced the emergence of monopoly positions on a global scale. And unfortunately, the stronger the monopoly position, the heavier the harm it inflicts on the society.

As explained in the previous sub-section, once a monopoly emerges one way or another, it is frequently inclined to start (or continue) to cheat to keep its position in the long run, through either rising barriers to entry by any means available (including those to fix regulations), or acquiring potential rivals before they can develop to become a threat, or starting price wars to wipe out weaker or developing rivals, or in other ways that are only limited by imagination. And in order to be able to do some or all of these without getting public opposition (which may eventually turn into a political demand by the society), it has to keep its monopoly status out of the scope of public awareness as much as possible as long as possible.

Although monopolies usually develop an expertise in hiding their harm to the society out of public attention, it is still not easy to stay in the shade forever without being detected. There are, however, other formations that are equivalent to monopolies in terms of destroying Fair Competition and harming the society through similar means, but are much harder to be detected by the Regulators and the society.

OLIGOPOLIES

When the concentration in a market increases such that practically a few competitors control most of the market, Fair Competition can be wiped out, although there is no single monopoly in sight and there are numerous competitors on the surface.

In cases where a few competitors dominate a market, they can practically mimic the behaviour of a monopoly, without even communicating with each other explicitly. Their common interests, like maximising their profits, and their collective power to effect or even set the market price (or conditions), enable them to do so. They collectively cheat against the customers and the society, and probably against their suppliers and the labour force, but not against each other.

It is of course possible that one of the members of an oligopoly may try to cheat against the others someday, however, that will ruin the unspoken cooperation between them as the others will follow suit, and start a new competition between them, eventually harming all. Therefore, unless one of the members feels that it can crush all the rest and become a permanent monopoly by itself, nobody will try to betray the unspoken alliance. For that reason, most sustainable oligopolies are made up of three to five competitors that have more or less the same strength in the market, but practically control the market by acting together.

Therefore, oligopolies are actually monopolies in disguise, with almost the same behavioural pattern and inflicting an equivalent damage on the wealth of the society. Moreover, they have a significant advantage for themselves. When they act as an oligopoly within a market with many other competitors, it is much easier to present the market as one where Fair Competition reigns and hide behind an image of fair winners in the eyes of both the society and the Regulators. Therefore, to maximise their success in hiding, oligopolies prefer many other smaller competitors without any practical market power to continue to exist in the market. This will easily deceit both the Regulators and the society, enabling oligopolies to enjoy most of the benefits of monopolies without the risk of becoming targets for anti-monopoly regulation and enforcement.

Regulators should therefore focus on any concentration of power in a market, and check to see whether competition is just an image on the surface or really exists in the market, primarily by checking how the prices and/or conditions are set in the market. If one or a few competitors are able to set prices or conditions, the existence of many competitors on the surface does not mean much.

In the rest of the discussion in the book, oligopolies will not be referred explicitly every time monopolies are mentioned, but just keep in mind that they are one and the same.

Monopolies And The Wealth Of The Society

Attaining a permanent monopoly status causes a change of behaviour in many ways.

The well known typical behaviour of a monopoly is fixing the market price at higher levels than that of a competitive market, without increasing the quality of the product or service, but just through decreasing the output, and thus increasing its profits at the expense of its customers.

Unfortunately, that is not the whole story. Relative to a competitive behaviour, a monopoly has at least two further hidden costs to the economy. First, it usually decreases investments and in turn the rate of productivity growth, which is good for its profits but bad for the long-term economic development of the society. And second, it usually utilizes its monopoly power in the markets where it is a major customer, paying less to both its suppliers and the labour force it utilizes.

All these types of behaviour, and many others not mentioned here, accumulate to a major misallocation of resources within the economy, decreasing the economic growth rate to way below its full potential and harming the welfare of the society in the long run.

CHANGES IN CONTRIBUTION VERSUS REWARD

The behaviour of a monopoly and the effects of such behaviour on the wealth of the society can alternatively be described from the viewpoint of contribution versus reward.

If the overall economy is simply viewed as a cake whose size varies depending on the contributions of the competitors in all markets within that economy, then a competitor's reward, namely its take of the cake, should be a portion of its contribution to the economy, namely a portion of the increase in the size of the cake that it creates. This way, the existence of that competitor creates a positive net benefit to the economy and to the wealth of the society.

Under Fair Competition, this net positive benefit to the economy will be maximized for each competitor. However, if a competitor becomes a monopoly, it simultaneously does two things: First, it will increase its reward significantly as the lack of competition leaves the society no chance to counter act that move. Second, it would not need and thus will not bother to increase its contribution to the maximum possible level, or may even keep it down deliberately to maximize its profit margin. Therefore, the monopoly does not only increase the size of its take of the cake, but also decreases the total size of the cake with respect to what it could have been under a fairly competitive environment.

Notice that this analysis is parallel to the analysis presented for cheating in Section 4.4, where it was explained that the loss of the rest of the society is much larger than the benefit of the Cheater, as the total wealth of the Cheater plus the rest of the society will fall due to cheating. Similarly, the loss of the rest of the society is much larger than the benefit of the monopoly, as the total wealth of the monopoly plus the rest of the society will fall due to its monopolistic behaviour. And this is only natural, as creating a permanent monopoly is practically the result of some sort of cheating, as explained in the previous sub-sections.

Unfortunately, even though the first part of the trouble, namely the monopoly's increasing its take of the cake too much, is somewhat recognized by the society, the second part of the trouble, namely the society's lagging its potential total size of the cake due to decreasing or disappearing competition, goes totally unrecognized, although it is actually the heavier part of the damage to the society's wealth in the long run. For this reason, societies with inadequate Social Intellect can not fully appreciate the vital importance of creating and keeping Fair Competition in their economy.

Innovation: Creating And Destroying Monopolies

INNOVATION CREATING MONOPOLIES

Innovation, which is mostly the fruit of heavy investment in research, is the driving force behind economic development in free markets. Moreover, as the economist Joseph Schumpeter argues, *competition based on innovation is more beneficial for the economy than competition based on pricing.* It is, therefore, for the best interest of the society to motivate companies to invest in research and innovation, by rewarding innovative success heavily.

In many cases a breakthrough innovation provides means to gain a temporary monopoly status for the innovative company, and such status, which enables the company to earn excessive profits as long as its monopoly status lasts, should be considered as a part of the financial reward to be given to motivate companies for innovative success. Such a temporary monopoly status is therefore good for the economy and the society in the long run.

The trouble, however, starts if and when the company enjoying the temporary monopoly status falls in love with the excessive profits associated with the monopoly status, and chooses to start to cheat in order to become a permanent monopoly. And when a company starts cheating from a temporary monopoly status, its chances of succeeding in becoming a permanent monopoly is much higher. As discussed above, if it succeeds, its appetite for further investment will diminish and its initial benefit to the society will turn into a long-term harm.

REGULATORS TO THE RESCUE

Once again, it is the duty of the Regulators to breakdown such permanent monopolies and enforce Fair Competition in the market. However, this is easier said than done when the monopoly status comes immediately after a breakthrough innovation.

The problems here are twofold. First, breakthrough innovations, like those that the societies have been experiencing with high tech companies during the latest decades, usually create a new type of market that the Regulator has little experience in, if any. The Regulator, therefore, faces major difficulty in deciding what the proper reaction should be. Second, if the company with the temporary monopoly status chooses to start cheating, its immediate target will be the Regulators themselves, who can then be guided relatively easily to unknowingly serve the interests of the monopoly rather than the society.

As it is impossible to develop a regulatory know-how before a new market appears, there is no easy escape from regulatory failure in the short run in such cases. The Regulators will at best catch up with the market after some delay, the length of which depends on the strength of the demand for Fair Competition by the society. And, the more intellectual the society, the stronger will be the demand, the shorter will be the delay in regulatory reaction, and the less will be the harm to the society. At the optimal case, the regulatory reaction will come fast enough to prevent any temporary monopolies turning into permanent ones, thus maximising the benefit of the society from innovation.

REWARDING INNOVATIVE SUCCESS: INTELLECTUAL PROPERTY

As innovation is the driving force behind economic development, it is for the best interest of the society to reward innovative success heavily. One common way of doing that is through intellectual property rights, which deliberately create a temporary monopoly status for the innovator, so that the innovator will make profits large enough to rationalize all the investment, hard work, time and effort it has devoted to research to come up with such innovation. Although the concept is straightforward, the trouble arises from the definition of *large enough*. The period during which an innovator keeps the intellectual property rights, namely the period during which the innovator will keep its monopoly status on the innovation, is supposed to bring excessive monopoly profits to the innovator as the reward of the innovation, at the expense of the society in the short run, based on the assumption that the benefit of such innovation for the society in the long run will dominate and there will eventually be a net benefit for the society. However, this very basic assumption makes sense if and only if the benefit of the innovator is fairly balanced against the benefit of the society through the proper fixation of the period of the intellectual property right by the Regulator. At that point, the issue gets further complicated, as the explicit financial expense of the society in terms of paying a higher price for that innovation during the monopoly period of the innovator is not the only cost to the society. A further implicit cost for the society that goes unnoticed, but one that is actually more significant, is the fact that, during the monopoly period granted to the innovator by the intellectual property right, other competitors who may build upon that innovation to develop further innovations are kept at the sides and any potential benefit for the society that may come from further innovations is therefore delayed and decreased, or even totally wasted. Therefore, the intellectual property period has to be fixed such that the benefit of the innovator versus the total explicit and implicit costs to the society should be fairly balanced. The monopoly status given to the innovator, should be long enough to fairly compensate for its innovative success, but should not be too long to create a net harm to the society in the long run.

And just as expected, any temporary monopoly trying to cheat its way into a permanent monopoly, would lobby on the Regulator to keep the intellectual property period long enough to give it ample time to become strong enough to erect high barriers to entry for other competitors. And accumulating such strength gets ever easier in today's integrated winner-takes-it-all markets, making the jobs of the Regulators ever more difficult.

Finally, even if the intellectual property period is tried to be fairly adjusted by the Regulator, due to the specific nature of a market, the time required for the fair compensation of the innovator may still be long enough to enable it to create high barriers to entry. In such cases, the Regulator has to step in once again later on, to break down any permanent monopoly and enforce Fair Competition. Unfortunately, in societies with inadequate Social Intellect, being an innovator is used as an effective defence against such anti-monopolistic moves, as an easily marketable idea to both the Regulators and the society. And the society pays the price in the long run.

INNOVATION DESTROYING MONOPOLIES – OR REPLACING THEM

Joseph Schumpeter introduced the concept of *creative destruction* which simply states that innovative companies will come to dominate a market wiping out their rivals. Such creative destruction may either come out of a jump in efficiency in the production of an existing product, or more commonly, through developing a totally new product that substitutes those of the rivals. Both cases, arising from leaps in innovation, wipe rivals out of the market, but benefits the society. In other words, creative destruction creates a net benefit for the society, as the total benefit of the innovator and the society outweighs the total loss of the competitors that were wiped out. Therefore, such leaps in innovation to enable creative destruction has to be supported by the society.

A further benefit for the society is that, creative destruction can be strong enough to wipe out the existing monopolies. However, for that to happen, the innovation should be so sudden and strong that the existing monopoly will be caught unguarded, which is not a common case. In many cases, when the existing monopoly detects the development of the new product or the production method, it simply buys out the innovative rival before it can challenge the monopoly. Or, the existing monopoly can heavily invest to attain similar developments, and through sacrificing some short-term profits, secures its position in the long-term. All these, however, require the existence of a strong monopoly and high barriers to entry. Once again, if the Regulator does a good job on decreasing barriers to entry, such creative destruction will have a higher chance of success at overthrowing the existing monopoly and thus increasing the welfare of the society.

However, although creative destruction may at times be sudden and strong enough to wipe out even the strongest monopolies, it can still not be the primary solution to eliminating permanent monopolies, for two reasons.

First, the stronger the existing monopoly, the more sudden and stronger the innovation and thus the forces of creative destruction have to be. This practically means that, *it may take a long time for a strong monopoly to be wiped out by creative destruction*, if ever. Therefore, *there will be too much time lost waiting for such innovation to come along, during which the existing monopoly will continue to harm the interests of the society.*

Second, and worse, *if the Regulator is failing to enforce Fair Competition in the market, any innovator that overthrows the existing monopoly through creative destruction, will itself become the next monopoly in the market.* And when one monopoly is replaced by another, there will not be much of a benefit for the society in the process.

Therefore, *even if creative destruction may work sooner or later, an intellectual society must still demand and support regulation for Fair Competition,* which includes the enforcement of anti-monopoly rules without delays, to minimize the harm given to the society by the monopolies.

Natural Monopolies

In principle, Free Market Economy requires that, in any market that can be open to competition, the state need not and should not participate, but just regulate properly to guard and enforce Fair Competition. Not all the markets, however, can be open to competition[19].

NATURAL MONOPOLIES BASED ON ECONOMIES OF SCALE

In some markets, economies of scale in production is vital to keep prices at optimal levels. In others, economies of scale in research and development is a necessity, as the cost of such research is too high and a potential waste of resources in parallel efforts would not be at the best interest of the society. In all such markets a lack of efficiency and/or innovation will cause a misallocation of resources. Therefore, due to the nature of these markets, the right solution may not be establishing Fair Competition, but rather allowing a monopoly status instead. These types of markets are called *natural monopolies* in the jargon.

Natural monopolies are a nightmare for the Regulator. On the one hand, breaking up monopolies in such markets will be against the best interest of the society. On the other hand, an under-regulated private monopoly would probably choose to have excessive profits at the expense of the society. No wonder why such markets are lucrative targets for Cheaters.

Therefore, in case of a necessity for a natural monopoly, the state must either dominate or participate in the production side, or if it chooses to stay out, must regulate the market much more closely and heavily, with respect to a competitive one. A regulatory failure in case of natural monopolies will inflict serious damage on the welfare of the society, so the Regulator has to identify a natural monopoly early, know the market very well, react very fast, regulate properly, and stay alert at all times. Although all these sound trivial, the practise can not fall further away from the principle.

NATURAL MONOPOLIES BASED ON NETWORK EFFECTS

The development of information and communications technology at breakneck speed in the latest decades has created networks on digital communication with a global reach, that constitute some new kind of natural monopoly.

These monopolies were not born out of cheating, but rather grew out of a competition based on merit in research and innovation. But the nature of these networks, in which *the winner-takes-it-all effect* is dominant, created a new beast within a very short period of time, namely *natural monopolies with a global span.*

What makes these a new type of monopoly is that, totally different from the classical monopolies that are mostly based on explicit financial interests, *these are based on a concentration of power on control over private data collection and information flow, and the processing of these through many algorithms, which implicitly contain financial interests that dwarf those of classic monopolies by orders of magnitude and has the potential to translate into global political power at a scale never experienced before.*

HIGH TECH MONOPOLIES ON DATA AND INFORMATION FLOW

High tech companies have this strange habit of offering their valuable services to all customers free of financial charge, namely money, and that is something that no society was conceptually prepared for, especially after decades of exposure to practical education on the virtue of getting financial rewards for any contribution to the society. This conceptually new approach, therefore, initially caught everybody off guard.

Years after the emergence and solid establishment of the monopolies based on high tech services, societies came to realize that these companies charge them in terms of a new currency, namely information. The trick with these companies is that, they come to control the flow of information both to and from their customers, such that,

- they extract personal data from the customer, which turns into a valuable asset once analysed through many algorithms, and can be used for many purposes spanning from economics to politics,

and,

- they control the flow of data to the customer, which turns into a valuable asset especially when combined with the analysis of the personal data of the customer, enabling the manipulation of customer opinion and perception on every imaginable dimension spanning from economics to politics.

As discussed in Book One of this series, once these monopolies gain the power to control information flow, they can potentially wipe out any person, any company, any product or any idea that they don't want the customer to have access to, and limit the information flow to their own interests, or to the interests of those they may be cooperating with, tailored through artificial intelligence to have maximum effect on the opinion and on the decisions of the customers. *At the most innocent cases, such power can be utilized to generate economic profits, while at more dangerous cases it can be used to manipulate political choices.* And *once the society loses its ability to freely access correct and complete information, there will be perfect information asymmetry - which will result in a total system failure in both economics and politics.*

Unfortunately, the failure of both the Regulators and the societies to recognize the potential dangers of the existence of such monopolies early in time, has significantly increased the cost of dealing with these monopolies today. However, considering the potential consequences, any society with adequate Social Intellect should be willing to pay the high price to break up such monopolies before it is too late.

As the first step, it is important to distinguish between the high tech companies that are really natural monopolies due to the network-based services they provide, versus those that are just regular monopolies that have emerged at a high speed due to their innovative products and then started to cheat to make their monopoly status permanent. In other words, *not all high tech companies are natural monopolies, but all prefer to hide behind that image.* To reemphasize, those that are natural monopolies have to be regulated closely and adequately, while those that are not natural monopolies have to be taken care of within an appropriate legal framework to reestablish competition in their respective markets.

However, for the enforcement of both these approaches, first their monopoly statuses have to be recognised by the Regulators.

Although the companies operating on high tech services have different characteristics in their nature that kept them out of the classic definition of monopolies, they could still have been diagnosed in time as a new type of monopoly if the concentration they created in the control of information flow were properly taken into account by the Regulators. Unfortunately, the failure of recognition of this new type of concentration has prevented the timely reaction of the Regulators. Meanwhile, these companies have easily achieved huge lobbying power directly over the Politicians thanks to their never-before-seen control over the flow of information, leaving any Regulator who may develop any awareness of the problem totally alone in his desperate struggle against them.

To cut the long story short, it took more than a decade, an infinitely long time compared to the speed of development and spread of these high tech monopolies, for the societies to realize the potential consequences of the problem and start to demand a solution from the Politicians and the Regulators. Hopefully sooner than later, the Lawmakers will start to think of and enforce regulations to reinstall Fair Competition where possible and to regulate closely where the natural monopolies can not be disintegrated. A starting point may be preventing these monopolies from buying out potential competitors and let creative destruction play its part. Fortunately, the forces of creative destruction are much stronger in high tech business with respect to other classic markets.

One particular trouble with these high tech monopolies is that they all have a global span, keeping them out of the enforcement power of any single Regulator, unless it cooperates with other Regulators in other societies. And this necessity may be a blessing in disguise for the global society, as it is time for every single society to realize that trying to achieve global economic and technological integration will bring more harm than good unless it is accompanied by some global cooperation on the political front – as will be discussed in a later book in this series.

Labour Markets

Most discussions on monopolies naturally focus on the supply side, namely on the producer monopolies that unfairly promote their own interests at the expense of their customers. However, there may as well be monopolies on the demand side that prevent Fair Competition in the markets they participate in as customers, this time promoting their own interests at the expense of their suppliers. And in many cases, major monopolies (or oligopolies) are practically monopolies on both sides, promoting their own interests at the expense of both their customers and their suppliers, maximising their harm to the welfare of the society.

MONOPOLIES IN LABOUR DEMAND

The problem of customer monopolies is most acute in the labour markets where all sorts of labour from unqualified to most qualified constitute the supply side, and a monopoly is the customer of such labour on the demand side. In such cases, the monopoly has total control over the demand for labour in that market and therefore can practically fix its price at an unfair level at the expense of the labour. Against such monopolised demand, unqualified labour may have a chance to relocate to other markets, but the trouble is much worse for the qualified labour where specific deep expertise is not that transferrable from one market to another.

In the recent decades, in most economically advanced societies, labour's share of the economic pie is continuously decreasing. The most widely advertised reasons for that are globalization and immigration, both being free flows of labour in essence, as either production goes to cheaper labour, or cheaper labour comes to production through immigration, to replace the expensive labour of the economically advanced societies. The free flow of labour is therefore one true reason, but it is not the only reason.

A second and a less discussed reason is that, rising automation and efficiency decreases the overall demand for masses of less qualified labour, especially in manufacturing industries. Although other new emerging businesses create some fresh demand, apparently their demand for less qualified labour is limited and can not balance the decreased demand due to automation, and as a result the price of less qualified labour falls.

A third and the best hidden reason is that, *the ever rising concentration and monopolization in many markets cause a concentration in the demand for both unqualified and qualified labour, decreasing the competition for labour, which in turn decreases the price of all sorts of labour, promoting the unfair interests of the monopolies at the expense of the labour.* These constitute market failures in every labour market in which monopolies exist, without any cure unless these monopolies are taken care of by the Regulators.

The wide-spread phenomenon of concentration of power in the markets, enabling the emergence of monopolies or oligopolies, therefore bring out the worst of all outcomes for the labour force. On the one hand, monopolies increase the price of their supply, namely their products and services, and everybody, including those who make a living on labour income, experience a decrease in their purchasing power as a customer. On the other hand, monopolies decrease the price of labour, and those who make a living on labour income experience a decrease in their earning power as labour. And when the two happens simultaneously, the trouble may reach unbearable levels for the labour force. And then the welfare of the society starts a deep dive, as will be discussed in Book Three of this series.

MONOPOLIES IN LABOUR SUPPLY

The formation of a labour union in a market is considered to be a way of counter balancing the forces that may drive down the price of labour, as they protect the rights of the labour and enable the labour not to settle for less than they deserve. And in principle labour unions serve this purpose well. However, in practise, it is also possible that these labour unions attain a high concentration in a market and become monopolies on the labour supply, to unfairly promote the interests of labour, such that they extract more than they deserve, at the expense of the companies that have a demand for labour while lacking any monopoly power as they happen to be in competitive markets. Such cases create another type of market failure in the labour market, resulting in a misallocation of resources at the expense of the welfare of the society.

FAIR COMPETITION IN THE LABOUR MARKET

Therefore, neither the lack of labour unions, nor an over-concentration that practically creates monopolies on the supply of labour, is good for the welfare of the society. For fair and optimal pricing in the labour market, there must be Fair Competition on both the supply and demand sides: just like the necessity of having many companies competing on the demand side for labour, there is a necessity for the existence of many labour unions competing on the supply side of labour too. It is this delicate balance that will maximise the welfare of the society.

Technology, Globalisation And The Rising Trend In Concentration Of Power

Although concentration of power is in the nature of Free Market Economy, the occurrence and spread of such cases were relatively limited until the recent decades. The developments in the latest decades, some of which are mentioned below, have significantly increased the cases of concentration of power within the overall economy, creating a major obstacle for the well-functioning of the economic system[20]. Notice that most of these developments are primarily based on the effects of technological advancements and/or globalisation.

- The establishment of *free trade* on a global basis, coupled with the advancement of *communication technologies* enabling global information flow between all producers and all consumers of any tradeable product, effectively merged the markets of many societies, creating *global markets* in many sectors. As the geographical barriers on trade and information flow evaporated, a *winner-takes-it-all effect* emerged in most globalised markets, as most customers channelled their demand to the best available producer in the global market. In the short run, it seems that a chance for all customers to reach the best product in a market is a blessing. However, this winner-takes-it-all effect heavily supports the emergence of concentrations of power, which in turn diminishes competition in the medium run and will eventually harm the customers.

- Developments in manufacturing technology, including *automation,* increased efficiency tremendously, creating higher barriers to entry for potential new competitors.

- Rising efficiency plays a more significant role whenever there are *economies of scale* in the nature of a sector. In such cases, when markets are integrated globally, their new vast scale amplifies the significance of efficiency and creates tremendous economies of scale, which in turn rises the barriers to unbreachable levels, virtually paving the way for the formation of global monopolies.

- The *free flow of labour enabled a relocation of high qualified labour through immigration towards the economically-advanced societies.* As a result, the competitors based in these economically-advanced societies have increased their research and development abilities. The resulting innovations in these competitors, accompanied by excessive intellectual property rights, created another great barrier to entry for any potential rivals in other societies, enabling these to become global monopolies once they can concentrate their power at home.

- *Free flow of capital* enabled global consolidation of companies through many mergers and acquisitions, creating concentrated powers in many markets, against which the regulating power of any government in any society fell short.

- The developments in information and communication technologies have created new types of *network economies,* which have a strong *winner-takes-it-all* nature, creating globally-spread monopolies within a very short time before any regulatory response can be formulated.

In principle, all these developments enable the creation of concentrations of power without any need for active cheating by any competitor *on an individual basis*. This, of course, does not mean that no competitor has ever cheated in practise. Remembering that no success can satisfy the greed in some, it does not require a genius to suspect that the speed and the scale of concentration of power have been further amplified in some cases through cheating at one stage or another.

On a collective basis, however, the situation is different. Most of the beneficiaries of concentrations of power based on the above developments, have guided the Politicians in their societies to enact laws and regulations that enabled the emergence of global trade and free flows of labour, capital, and information. When globalisation materializes without Fair Competition on a global basis, all the beneficiaries that concentrate their power in their markets are actually cheating simultaneously against all the societies, including their own. From another viewpoint, the first and third conditions for Fair Competition presented in Section 2.2 were passively violated by most competitors during globalisation, thus, there is significant cheating against all the societies that will reveal its negative effects in the long run.

The New-born Trouble With Monopolies : Local vs Global Competition

In principle, it is for the best interest of a society to establish Fair Competition in all its markets and prevent any over-concentration of economic power in any of them. And in any market closed to global competition this principle works fine in practise. But if a market is open to global competition, existential troubles may emerge in practise.

Consider the integration of markets among societies all of which adhere to the principles of Fair Competition. If these societies integrate their markets, there will be more but still fair competition in these new integrated markets, and in the long run a better allocation of resources will emerge within the integrated economies of all these societies. In this theoretical case, therefore, integration of markets is a wise move. Unfortunately, this theoretical case is far away from the reality of our day.

Consider the case with a group of societies, with different economic sizes, where some societies adhere to Fair Competition in their local markets while others let (or even support) monopolies to emerge and survive in theirs. If the markets in all these societies are integrated into a global market, the rest of the story may flow differently.

The concentrated economic power of the monopolies in some of these societies, especially when these societies have huge markets compared to the others, may dominate the economic power of the many fair competitors from the other societies in this new global market. Therefore, these initially local monopolies may eventually wipe out the fair players in the new global market and become global monopolies. And, needless to say, the stronger the global monopoly, the higher the damage it will inflict on all the societies.

Therefore, if the integration of markets proceeds with high speed but with little wisdom and caution, as it has happened in the recent decades, the societies that have prevented concentrations of economic power within their local markets will face a great trouble in protecting their local competitors against the fierce and unfair competition coming from the monopolies of some other societies. In this case where unwise and ill-structured globalisation emerged, the fair competitors from some societies will be forced to face the monopolies of the others and be crushed by them, and thus globalisation will heavily hurt the wealth and welfare of the societies that had prevented concentration of power before integration. To reemphasize, global monopolies that may emerge will eventually hurt all the societies, but they will hurt those with competitive-markets-before-integration more than those with monopolies-before-integration.

There are two practical precautions to prevent this catastrophic outcome.

The first, but the dangerous solution, is to let concentration of economic powers to emerge and to survive in all societies before and during integration, so that local monopolies will compete against other local monopolies when the markets are integrated. If the global society is extremely lucky, none of the competitors in this clash may dominate the others, and the new global market will be based on some sort of competition, denying the position of a global monopoly to any of the local monopolies. In other words, by integrating markets globally, all societies will effectively convert their locally-monopolised markets into a globally-competitive market. Unfortunately, this sounds too good to be true for all markets. Most probably, in many markets, one of the competing local monopolies will crush all the rest and become a global monopoly, with the catastrophic consequences mentioned before for all societies.

The second, but wiser solution, is not to integrate all markets in all societies globally, but to limit the scope of integration with only the markets where there is no concentrated power in any society. But, as discussed before, the existence or non-existence of concentration of economic power is usually an economy-wide phenomenon in practise. Therefore, *societies that enforce competitive markets and prevent concentrations of power in their economies may create an integrated market among themselves, again with no concentration of power after integration (thus, keeping the best interest of all the societies), and do not integrate societies that tolerate or create monopolies until they change behaviour.*

Different approaches can also be utilised on a market basis initially, but only temporarily, combining the two mentioned above. But the crucial issue is that, *the current approach to globalisation is not well structured and must be significantly modified before proceeding further in the long run.* And, as preventing or dissolving monopolies in some markets while keeping those in others is not a workable strategy for global integration, *fighting against concentration of power must become a global understanding and approach, before any real progress can be made towards worldwide integration. And that, unfortunately, does not seem to be easy.*

The details of appropriate approaches to globalisation will be discussed in a later book in this series.

5.3   Over-Competition And Zombies

Over Competition: The Hidden Disease

The well established but misunderstood belief regarding competition is that, the higher the competition the better and the cheaper will be the resulting products (or services). This is true in cases where a market is newborn and initially has less than optimal competition. A rise in competition in such under-competitive markets is a desired development that is highly beneficial for the society. As time passes, more competitors join the market, drive down the initial high profit margins and increase the quality of the output. Eventually, competition will reach its optimal level in the market, such that the competitors will have optimal profitability (as will be explained below) while their output will have an optimal price to quality balance. Any further increase in competition beyond this optimal level will then start to hurt both the competitors and their customers, as well as the society at large. Unfortunately, sometimes new competitors continue to enter a market where there is already optimal competition and cause a further rise in competition which will do more harm than good for all.

What Happens When Over-Competition Arises

COMPETITION AND PROFITABILITY

In an optimal competition that will benefit the society in the long run, the competitors in a market should have not-too-high-but-positive average profit margins in the medium run. The critical term here is medium-run-profitability. The medium run in an economy contains sunshine, namely periods of strong economic performance, rain, namely periods of weak economic performance, and once in a while, thunder, namely periods of economic hardship or crisis. A healthy medium-run-profitability requires having a positive profit margin at all times except those of thunder. This will mean a relatively higher profit margin in the sunshine, and a relatively lower but still positive margin in the rain. Only in this way the accumulated profits of companies at times of sunshine and rain, will enable them to survive through the thunder.

In cases where new competitors join a market that already has enough (optimal) competition, over-competition will arise in the market. And when there is over-competition in the market, many competitors in the market lose medium-run-profitability. They may still make some profits under sunshine, but eat away those under rain, and face huge and usually fatal losses when the thunder comes. Such widespread failures in a market frequently turn into a too-important-to-sacrifice problem whose burden will eventually be borne by the society – as discussed in Section 3.3.

WHAT HAPPENS WHEN THERE IS OVER-COMPETITION

Times of thunder clearly reveal the heavy harms of over-competition on the competitors and the society. Unfortunately, the harms of over-competition do not wait for a thunder, or even rain, to effect the market and the economy. Even at times of sunshine, over-competition hurts the market, although such harm may remain well hidden for a long time.

In the simplest form, a competitor makes some operational profits, then pays interest to its debtholders (creditors, bond holders, etc.), and on whatever is left, pays taxes to the state. What remains after all those is the net profit of its shareholders. In this regard, a healthy competitor in an optimally-competitive market should be able to create some net profits for its shareholders at times of both sunshine and rain, and keep some of those within the company as reserves for days of thunder that are sure to come sooner or later.

When competition increases too much within a market, the weakest competitors in the market start to suffer first. As they try to compete through decreasing prices, their profit margins start to erode. What usually follows is a sacrifice of their future, through decreasing research and development efforts, to decrease their costs, with the hope to recover margins in the short run. When this fails too, they may next start to take irrational and excessive risks, as they start to feel that they have nothing left to lose, and try to gain a competitive edge out of risk taking, praying for luck. All such changes in their behaviour may necessitate some rival competitors to mimic that behaviour to keep their short-term competitive edge, spreading the harm to others. As over-competition continues, these weakest competitors will next lose their ability to make their interest payments to their debtholders, which is the sign of the beginning of the end for them. In many cases, however, the debtholders will try to keep such competitors alive (rather than immediately driving them to bankruptcy) by delaying their demand for appropriate payment, with the hope that these competitors may survive someday and make a full payment rather than a partial one. This chain of developments creates the so-called *zombie companies*. Unless luck intervenes unexpectedly, these zombies will eventually lose their ability to make any operational profits at all, and meet their destinies. The trouble here is that, the longer some competitors survive in a zombie-state, the more they sustain the over-competitive environment in the market, causing damage to the other competitors. They may even drag some competitors which would have survived under optimally-competitive conditions, to failure with themselves.

Under a relatively good scenario, some markets may survive these over-competitive periods, and as the zombies eventually leave the market and the competition decreases towards optimal levels again, the stronger competitors will re-establish their medium-run-profitability, preventing a total market failure.

Unfortunately, the relatively good scenario is not the common one. In a worse but more realistic and common scenario, the zombies stay alive longer than the rest of the competitors can bear, or new competitors continue to arrive (for reasons to be discussed later in this section) to replace the departing zombies and keep the environment over-competitive for a too long time.

When the environment remains over-competitive in a market for a long time, all the competitors, including the strongest and the most merited ones, start to lose profitability, even at times of sunshine. This will cause some competitors to desperately revert to cheating against their rivals to gain some competitive advantage. But, as discussed before, when some competitors start to cheat, others have no choice but to start cheating as well to stay competitive. And when all cheat together against each other, none will get any sustainable competitive advantage against others. Therefore, the competitors on the supply side will next start to cheat all together against their customers and the society, to somewhat improve their profit margins. However, it won't take long for over-competition to drive all those margins to zero or below, again. In short, if over-competition stays alive for a too long time, all competitors in a market will lose profitability and become sorts of zombies, and a total market failure will follow. And if the market is a strategic one whose existence is vital for the society, the society will have to bear all the burden of this failure financially, and will have to re-establish the market with better regulation this time. And in the unfortunate but still common cases where optimal regulation does not accompany the re-establishment of the market, the same chain of events will result in a similar market failure sooner or later. That is to say, until the society manages to rise its Social Intellect to cease repeating the same mistakes over and over again.

OVER-COMPETITION AND MISALLOCATION OF RESOURCES

All through the chain of events discussed above, a series of misallocation of resources emerge: when some competitors start taking excessive risks, when cheating starts in desperation and spreads within the market, when debtholders keep some resources buried in zombies while such resources might have been channelled elsewhere for better use, when some competitors who would have survived in an optimally competitive market fail due to the emergence of over-competition, when the society bears the burden of saving some too-important-to-sacrifice markets, etc. Over-competition, therefore, is a destroyer of the wealth and welfare of the society.

Why Do Markets Become And Stay Over-Competitive

The main reason for over-competition to arise and survive is the continuous arrival of new competitors, who are willing to take higher risks for lower returns, to markets where there is already high enough (optimal) competition. When these newcomers arrive, the risks that all competitors have to take rise, while their profit margins fall. Starting from the weakest competitors, this worsening of the risk versus return characteristic of the market drives all the competitors towards becoming zombies. And the rest of the story goes as explained above.

The crucial question, therefore, is why and how these newcomers who accept lower returns for higher risks emerge? And what forces them to behave that way?

The reason for this undesired phenomenon that ruins the markets and heavily harms the wealth of the society will be discussed in detail in Section 5.4. But before that, some other reasons that create and sustain over-competition, many of which usually exist simultaneously, have to be examined.

NEWCOMERS MISCALCULATING EXPECTED OUTCOMES

As explained in Section 3.2, any rational investor first makes a forecast on the potential outcome of his planned investments and then makes his final decision. And the success of these forecasts heavily depends on the knowledge and experience of the forecaster on the market. Naturally, the knowledge and experience of the newcomers are relatively much less then those competitors who have already been in the market for a long time. It follows that, the newcomers make worse forecasting mistakes in making their investment decisions. But any investment decision based on such miscalculations, when realised, will eventually hurt all the competitors in the market as the newcomer will definitely rise the competition in the market. Therefore, the higher the number of newcomers, the more is the creation of over-competition and the more will be the number of zombies born.

THE CUMULATIVE OVER INVESTMENT PROBLEM

Any market, in which most or all of the competitors earn sustainable and satisfying profits under the current conditions, naturally attracts further investment, not only from the newcomers but also from the existing competitors. A common trouble is, each competitor, on his own, makes a forecast on how much additional profits some additional investment will bring, with the implicit assumption that he will be the first to make the investment and grab the potential profits, and the others will not be fast enough to react until it is too late. Although the forecast can be correct under this hidden assumption, the assumption itself is unrealistic. What happens in practise is that, too much investment will be made simultaneously, by too many competitors sharing the same wrong assumption. And when the cumulative investment is so high with respect to the remaining potential in the market, the market becomes over-competitive.

EGOS OR HEAVY INITIAL INVESTMENTS CREATING HIGH BARRIERS TO EXIT

In some cases, a potential competitor exaggerates its own abilities and strengths, miscalculates the expected outcome of his potential investment, and under optimistic expectations joins a market where he can not succeed. However, even when it becomes clear that the business is not going as expected, and that failure is inevitable in the medium run, many competitors still deny the fact that their initial forecast and/or practical execution has failed, and insist to go on with the failing business. This is a common case especially when the operations can be somehow financed in the short-run, although a -currently unrecognised or denied- heavy operational loss is inevitable in the long run. And the situation gets even worse if there were heavy initial investments that have already become sunk costs.

In cases where there is a high level of initial cash capital, or the shareholders may be willing to pour good money after bad, or the competitor can still borrow from the banks, or the failing competitors are supported by the state or by the policies of the state institutions, there may be enough cash to keep the business alive in the short run. In the meantime a heavy loss arises either from a heavy initial investment that is illiquid or has no market value left, and/or from the accumulation of heavy liabilities incurred during the ongoing operations. The recognition of this heavy loss is usually delayed with the desperate hope that a miracle may happen and good luck will save the business.

Well known examples of zombies common in such cases are the banks or companies that have enough liquidity to pay for their liabilities in the short-term and thus stay alive for a little longer, but are actually insolvent in the sense that their assets have already fallen to inadequate levels to cover their liabilities in the long-term.

The longer these zombie companies stay alive, the heavier the eventual loss becomes, making the recognition of it ever more difficult until the business inevitably collapses and/or goes bankrupt. But until eventual failure, the zombie company will stay in the competition, almost always applying desperate irrational pricing or conditions to stay alive, creating over-competition and harming the rest of the competitors and the market.

THE SIMULTANEOUS LOCK IN

As competition starts to increase in a market, the medium-term profitability of many or all competitors may fall below sustainable levels. However, if the eventual losers are not crystal clear as the competitors are of similar strength, and if all competitors know that once some of them leave the market the remaining ones will become profitable again, all will do their best to stay alive beyond the others' horizon of survival. The trouble here is that, their horizons of survival may also be similar, driving all of them to eventual failure simultaneously. Unless some mergers or acquisitions solve the problem and restore profitability, such persistence will sustain over-competition, and may eventually cause a market failure.

EXCESSIVE RISK TAKERS

At times of sunshine, especially when it lasts for too long, some newcomers or some existing competitors may get too optimistic in their forecasts and take excessive risks, beyond any rational calculation. This will force the other competitors in the market to mimic such behaviour at least up to some extent, to stay competitive. When the rain comes eventually all competitors will have to face huge losses, and at best, the excessive risk taker will drag many others out of the market with itself. The even worse but common case is that, all competitors succeed to stay in the market till the thunder arrives, and then they will all collapse simultaneously, creating a market failure whose burden will most probably fall on the society.

MIS-REGULATION

While trying to keep markets away from over-concentration or monopolization, namely against an environment of under-competition, the Regulators may sometimes mis-analyse the situation in a market. In certain cases, like a period following an innovative breakthrough in the market, or the periods of sunshine in the overall economy, many companies enjoy high profit margins. This does not necessarily mean that they are becoming permanent monopolies or oligopolies. There may be a monopoly problem only if high profit margins persist in the long run, including the rainy days. However, if the regulator overreacts to the high profit margins at the days of innovation or sunshine, it may decrease barriers to entry too much, or exaggerate regulatory changes or enforcement, and this time pave the way for harmful over-competition.

ZOMBIES KEPT ALIVE BY FINANCIAL INSTITUTIONS

In principle, the failing competitors, namely the companies that lost their ability to service their debt payments, are supposed to go bankrupt and leave the market. In practise, however, their debtholders, namely the banks and other financial institutions, may prefer to keep them alive as zombies, by delaying their demand for appropriate payment. One reason for that is the hope that these zombies may recover someday and payback their debt in full. Another equally important reason is that, if the financial institutions recognize the failure of these companies, they will have to reflect the loss from these companies to their own financial statements, decreasing their capital adequacy ratios, necessitating their shareholders to inject further capital. At days of thunder, this is the last thing they would want to do, thus, they prefer to keep a closed eye on the situation and just roll over the unpaid debt. This will not only sustain over-competition in the relevant markets and harm them, but also will keep valuable resources locked-in at those zombie companies rather than allocating them to healthy borrowers, causing a major misallocation of resources in the overall economy, further harming the welfare of the society.

ZOMBIES KEPT ALIVE BY CENTRAL BANK OR GOVERNMENT POLICIES

At times of thunder, on the one hand, zombies emerge more frequently and widely throughout the whole economy, while on the other hand, both the central banks and the governments adjust their policies to improve market conditions and support the economy. As a side effect of such policy changes, both the existing and the newborn zombie companies get the chance to survive longer.

When the central banks change their monetary policies and decrease interest rates, on the one hand, they may refuel economic growth up to some extent, but on the other hand, by decreasing the interest payment liabilities of the zombie companies, they enable them to go unnoticed and survive longer. Similarly, when governments adopt fiscal policies to supply stimulus to the economy at times of thunder, they also enable the zombie companies to survive much longer.

The survival of the zombies, however, counterbalance the short-term positive effects of such policies in the long-term, as valuable resources like capital and labour will stay locked in the zombies. In other words, what usually happens is that, such policy changes solve some short-term problems like weakening bank balance sheets or rising unemployment, only to transform them into other bigger problems that will arise in the long-term.

Unfortunately, as such policies are heavily demanded by the society (more for social reasons rather than economic wisdom) at times of economy-wide troubles, it is practically impossible to eliminate them completely. Therefore, the solution lies at minimising the emergence of the zombie companies before and during the times of economy-wide troubles.

The primary reason for the emergence of the zombie companies is the existence of over-competition in the markets. And such over-competition emerges under normal economic conditions and thus already exists before any economy-wide troubles arise. Therefore, the crucial question here is *why do many markets become over-competitive simultaneously under normal economic conditions?* Again, the answer is in Section 5.4.

Over-Competition In Labour Markets

Just like in any other market, there can be over-competition on the supply side of the labour markets. Such over-competition arises when too much labour chases too few employment opportunities. In other words, over-competition arises when the labour supply is too large with respect to the labour demand.

The nature of the labour markets, however, is much different than the rest, at least for the fact that the labour markets can not be let to misfunction, let alone fail, for social, economic and political reasons.

When labour markets are taken on a micro-basis, namely on a product or service sector basis, some micro-labour-markets may weaken or even totally disappear in time, while others emerge or strengthen simultaneously. In other cases, the price of labour or the working conditions in some micro-markets may worsen, while those in others get better. As long as there is some general mobility between micro-labour-markets, such that the labour supply in one market can relocate in reaction to the decrease in the labour demand in that market or the increase in the labour demand in some other market, the macro-balances in the overall labour market may remain healthy and socially acceptable.

Under those conditions, whenever the labour demand in some micro-market falls while that in another rises, labour relocates from one micro-market to the other, and the balance between the labour supply and labour demand in the overall labour market remains socially acceptable, in the sense that unemployment will be within acceptable limits and labour can earn a decent income in line with its qualifications, working under acceptable conditions.

At times when a specific micro-market where the labour force is incapable of immediately relocating to other micro-markets for certain reasons, fails or disappears, the social security system of the society can take care of the unemployed labour until a long-term solution can be found.

In short, even though problems may arise within micro labour markets, the macro labour market will function properly as long as

- there is enough mobility between micro labour markets,
- the demand and supply of labour is somewhat balanced in the macro labour market, such that the price of labour (with respect to its qualification) will not fall to unacceptable levels, and
- there is adequate competition on both the supply and demand sides of the macro labour market, such that no one on any side can dictate the price of labour and/or the conditions under which labour will be employed.

Naturally, each of these conditions may fail from time to time, but as long as the failure is temporary, the social security system of the society may handle the situation well without causing any wide-spread social unease in the society.

However, when the second and/or the third conditions fail and stay that way for the long run, social troubles are on the horizon.

By the nature of the labour markets, the price of labour should not fall below a certain level, as most members of the society live by selling their physical or mental labour, and there is a minimum limit their income need to stay above to have a decent life. As mentioned above, if a few number of people (with respect to the size of the society) fall below that limit for a temporary period, the social security system can help them out. However, if too many people need the help of the social security system for a too long time, at best they will be a huge burden on the society, and at worst, the social security system will collapse. Either way, social peace will be in danger.

Therefore, the reasons for the failure of the two conditions mentioned above must be well understood, and precautions have to be taken to minimise the chances of emergence and/or the duration of such failures, to protect the welfare of the society.

The second condition above, namely the balance of demand and supply in the macro labour market, can fail for many well known reasons. At times of economic slowdown, the macro demand for labour and therefore its price falls. When technological developments enable more automation, especially in production sectors, the demand for labour falls.

The rise of the share of high-tech services within the economy, which utilise only a limited amount of high qualified labour, remains inadequate to counter balance any significant fall in labour demand. The moving of production plants to other societies where the labour price is much lower, decreases the demand for labour in the local markets. Immigration of all sorts increase the labour supply in the macro market. The list may go on forever, but the bottom line is that when the macro demand for labour falls while the macro supply of labour rises, the price (and working conditions) of labour will deteriorate fast towards unacceptable levels. These dynamics are somewhat understood, at least in the economically developed western societies, and thus a political demand for counter measures can be expected to rise in time.

The third condition, namely the need for competition on the demand side of the labour markets, is much less understood. In micro levels, when monopolies (or concentrations of power) arise in some markets, the demand side for labour in those markets become uncompetitive. For practical purposes, this will cause a deterioration in both the working conditions and the price of labour in those micro labour markets. Assuming some labour mobility, this will cause a shift of labour force towards other micro labour markets where pricing and conditions are better, effectively increasing the labour supply in those markets. This in turn will somewhat deteriorate the labour prices and working conditions in those markets as well, spreading the trouble. In short, the monopolisation of some markets, will initially harm the labour markets of their own, but afterwards, will cause an increase the labour supply in the other markets and thus will harm the labour markets of those markets as well – even though the demand side in those labour markets may still be competitive. And when monopolisation and concentration of power spreads to many markets within the economy, their cumulative effect will eventually harm the macro labour market of the society. In other words, *when under-competition spreads on the demand side of the macro labour market, the supply side of the macro labour market will effectively face over-competition, which in turn will deteriorate the price and working conditions of all the labour force in the society.*

5.4   Under-Competition, Over-Competition, And Their Interaction

A Vital Observation

As discussed in Section 5.2, when concentration of economic power emerges in a particular market, the competition in that market decreases. And when concentration rises further and becomes a monopoly (or an oligopoly), there is very little competition left in that market. This is well recognised by all societies as a clear case of under-competition.

What is not so well recognised but actually more important, is that, *while the emergence of concentration of power means under-competition for the monopoly in that market, it corresponds to extreme-over-competition for any other existing competitor or potential newcomer.* This is simply because, the absolute dominance of the monopoly in that market does not let any other existing competitor or potential newcomer to have any meaningful market share or to earn any profits even if they take excessive risks.

Contagion Of Over-Competition

Free capital, whether it belongs to an existing competitor or a newcomer, analyses the potential returns (profit margins) versus the risks in many markets simultaneously before making a new investment decision. As there is no return even for excessive risk takers in a monopolised market (except for the monopoly itself), new investments will naturally stay away from such markets. In other words, free capital will not flow to markets that present extreme-over-competition for any competitor except the monopoly. Not only newcomers will prefer other markets, but existing competitors will search for liquidating their investments (mostly through selling to the monopoly) and leave for other markets as well. After all, nobody wants to become a zombie.

Naturally, the most attractive investment targets for free capital come out to be the competitive markets, where profit margins are much higher and risks are much lower compared to the monopolised markets.

As explained in Section 5.3, when new capital flows into a market, either because of the entry of newcomers or because of the new investments of the existing competitors, competition in that market will rise. As a result, profit margins will fall and risks will rise, worsening the return versus risk characteristic in that market for all competitors.

Free capital, even if it belongs to a newcomer, is mostly bright enough to realise that when it flows into a market it will worsen the existing return versus risk characteristic, by both decreasing returns and increasing risks. However, this natural change is irrelevant to the investment decision. What matters is where the free capital will find the best return versus risk characteristic among the existing competitive markets, following its entry. *As the markets dominated by monopolies already offer terrible return versus risk characteristics, the characteristic in a currently competitive market, even after it will be worsened by the entry of the new capital, looks very attractive in comparison. To answer the first question asked in Section 5.3, this is exactly why newcomers accepting to take higher risks for lower returns arrive in the competitive markets, consequently rising competition in these markets too.*

Therefore, the existence of monopolies in some markets, will promote higher risk taking for lower returns in newcomers and directs them to other currently competitive markets, to consequently drive these markets towards over-competition.

In other words, *the existence of extreme-over-competition for new capital in monopolised markets, drives free capital to the other ones that look relatively much less competitive with better margins, eventually rising the competition and decreasing the margins in them too.*

Needless to say, capital continuously flows from more competitive markets towards less competitive markets, and therefore, the return versus risk characteristics in all markets tend to level out in the medium run. What this means in practise is that, the higher the number and scale of monopolised markets with terrible return versus risk characteristics for free capital (for newcomers), the more the new capital will flow to other currently competitive markets, and thus the higher will rise the number of markets with over-competition and zombies[21]. In short, *over-competition is highly contagious even between completely irrelevant markets. And this answers the second question asked in Section 5.3, namely why many markets become over-competitive simultaneously under normal economic conditions.*

It directly follows that, *the protection of an optimal level of competition in one market necessitates the protection of optimal level of competition in the other markets. And that is terrible news for every Regulator in every market, as the success of one depends on the success of the others.*

CONTAGION FROM THE VIEWPOINT OF OVERALL MARKET DEMAND

A monopoly charges higher prices for its product (with respect to the case of perfect competition), such that, although it may face some decrease in demand, its total income and profits will be higher. This will practically mean that, in most cases, it will eventually get a higher proportion of the overall consumption budget of the society, as those customers who continue to consume that product will be allocating a higher percentage of their individual budget to that product. Therefore, the remaining consumption budget of those customers for other products in other markets will fall, decreasing the overall demand for other products in other markets.

Moreover, as the rise of the monopoly will cause a misallocation of resources, the total wealth and therefore the overall consumption budget of the society will fall. What this means is that, the consumption budget of the customers who never had any interest in the monopoly's market will fall as well. And this will further decrease the overall demand for other (totally irrelevant) products in other markets.

Therefore, *the rise of the monopoly (on the supply side) in one market will simultaneously hurt all the producers (on the supply sides) of other markets sooner or later.*

In Conclusion

The analyses in this section reveal that, while the emergence of concentration of power in a market means under-competition for the monopoly in that market, it corresponds to extreme-over-competition for any other existing competitor in that market or for any potential newcomer to that market. For that reason, free capital prefers to flow to the currently competitive markets, consequently rising competition in these markets too. This makes over-competition highly contagious even between completely irrelevant markets, and for that reason, many markets become over-competitive simultaneously under normal economic conditions. Therefore, to prevent the spread of over-competition in an economy, the first step should be to prevent the emergence of monopolies in any market.

As discussed, the spread of over-competition creates a terrible misallocation of resources within the overall economy and harms the wealth and welfare of the society in the long run. It is therefore critical whether the society increases its Social Intellect fast enough to realise the potential harm to be caused by the concentration of economic power (or monopolisation) in some markets and the emergence of over-competition in other markets as a consequence.

The potential harm will get worse when the scope and the speed of the rise in monopolisation and the resulting spread of over-competition are higher. Unfortunately, this comes out to be the case when the major markets (where a significant portion of the overall economic value within a society are created) are monopolised first, mostly with the aid of some political support. It will then require a short period of time for over-competition to spread through all the rest of the relatively minor markets, and complete the damage. And if all these occur before the society can develop adequate Social Intellect to resist or reverse the change, concentrated economic powers will team up with concentrated political power, to permanently keep their status and promote their own interests against those of the society.

Therefore, the discussion will inevitably shift to politics in the coming chapters.

Chapter 6

LAWMAKERS AND CHEATERS

6.1   Cheating, Regulation And Enforcement

Authority Versus Chaos

Centuries ago, English philosopher Thomas Hobbes argued that the society can either live in a world-of-law where there is some authority, or in a world-of-chaos if there is no authority. In this very simple but still valid logic, the authority (preferably one that is legitimate) has two complementary functions: it makes law and it enforces law.

Avoiding The Enforcement Of Law

Reflecting this framework to competition and cheating in Free Market Economies, each competitor has two options:

- He may abide by the law, either because he is ethically willing to do so, or because he knows that the law will be enforced on him anyway,

  or,

- he may cheat as he believes that the law can not be enforced on him, either because the authority is too ignorant or too weak to do so, or worse, because the authority will protect him, betraying the society, to directly or indirectly share the benefits of his cheating.

From the viewpoint of the argument of Hobbes, the Cheaters are actually introducing a bit of chaos into the world-of-law. The trouble is that, once some competitors start doing so, others may follow soon. Then, chaos will start to spread and dominate what was once a world-of-law, and eventually destroy it completely to create a complete world-of-chaos, which in turn will harm all of the society, including the Cheaters themselves.

The wise Cheaters are therefore aware that, for them to gain a net benefit from cheating, both against their rivals in their own market and against the society at large, two conditions have to be met simultaneously:

- They should be able to cheat themselves in their own market, and thus the law should not be enforced on them, and,
- the other competitors (in their own market or in other markets) must not be able to cheat, so that there will not be a world-of-chaos, thus, the law must be enforced on others.

Only in this way the Cheaters can have a net benefit from introducing elements of chaos to the world-of-law, harming the rest of the society.

FALLACY OF CHEATING, REVISITED

The discussion above, based on the framework of Hobbes, is actually nothing but presenting the basic concept of *fallacy of cheating* introduced in Section 4.4 from a different viewpoint. In any market, cheating brings a competitive advantage and thus a net benefit only when a few competitors cheat and most of the others do not or can not. If every competitor cheats in a market, nobody gains any competitive advantage against any other, and no one gets a benefit from cheating, while still harming the rest of the society. And if cheating spreads to all the markets, the overall conversion to a world-of-chaos will have a net harm on every competitor in every market.

In light of this fact, the aim of each Cheater needs to be somehow guiding the Regulators to neglecting his cheating while enforcing the regulations on others throughout the economy. Achieving this, unfortunately for the Cheaters, and fortunately for the society, is neither easy nor sustainable in practice. And the more so, the higher the Social Intellect of the society. The Cheaters, then, have to develop a better approach.

Influencing The Making Of Law

If equal and widespread enforcement of laws and regulations can not be avoided, the only choice left for the Cheater is to influence the Lawmakers and Regulators, and make sure that the laws and regulations are made in such a way that they benefit only the Cheater and not the rest of his rival competitors, so that the enforcement of such law on the whole market will be just fine for the Cheater. Moreover, as a welcome side effect for the Cheater, widespread enforcement of law will give the impression of having a Fair Competition in the market.

Once again, if a Cheater can influence the making of laws and regulations regarding his own market, other Cheaters in other markets can also do so in their markets. This will again result in an overall harm for the whole society, and may wipe out the benefit of the Cheater in his own market and result in a net overall loss.

A wise Cheater, therefore, is aware of the critical issue here: *the law he influences should so heavily benefit the Cheater that, even though similar ill-designed laws may benefit other Cheaters in other markets and harm him as a member of the society, his net overall benefit must still remain positive.* In other words, the benefit he gets out of the influenced-law-to-his-advantage in his own market should be so huge that, it will more than offset all the aggregate negative harm of all the other wise Cheaters in all the other markets inflicted upon him as a member of that society. From the viewpoint of the concentrated-benefits-distributed-costs phenomenon of Section 4.2, this corresponds to the case where the wise Cheater's concentrated benefit in his own market outweighs all the aggregate distributed costs inflicted on him by the other Cheaters in other markets.

Any wise Cheater who may succeed to do so becomes a hidden member of the *Cheating Elite* – a minority group of Cheaters who manage to attain huge overall net benefits to themselves, in spite of the existence of the other Cheaters (and the rest of the Cheating Elite) throughout the economy, naturally at the expense of the society.

Most Cheaters, however, can only exert a limited influence on the Lawmakers and Regulators (through the ways discussed in Chapter 4), and only manage to attain marginal benefits in their own markets, thus unknowingly face a net loss due to the harm inflicted on them by the other Cheaters in other markets. Unfortunately, all such Cheaters still inflict a heavy aggregate loss on the society, and thus are as harmful as the Cheating Elite.

REGULATIONS AT MICRO LEVELS VERSUS LAWMAKING AT MACRO LEVELS

The process of lawmaking and regulation spans a continuous spectrum, starting from the Politicians at the Legislative and the Executive bodies, all the way to the Regulators at the depths of the state bureaucracy. For the discussion of influencing lawmaking, it is necessary to differentiate between the economy-wide laws at macro-levels enacted by the Politicians versus the market specific regulations at micro-levels mostly enacted by the Regulators.

INFLUENCING REGULATIONS AT MICRO LEVEL

Market specific regulations aim to promote the conditions of Fair Competition at the market level, including the protection of consumers against market specific asymmetries of information and the society against market specific externalities. The Cheaters that compete in different markets, therefore, have different interests towards which they try to influence the regulations. The crucial point here is that, they only need to deal with the relevant Regulators in their own specific markets to achieve their goals.

All Cheaters, from the naivest to the wisest, try to influence the regulations to their own benefit at the expense of the other competitors and the society. If they succeed, the Regulators will be serving their purposes either through failing to enact the necessary regulations (and enable the Cheaters to cheat easily) or mis-regulating the market to the benefit the Cheaters. Then, the resulting un-regulated or mis-regulated free competition creates concentrations of power in their specific markets, and destroys perfect competition - and therefore also destroys Fair Competition by definition.

In trying to exert such influence, the Cheaters utilise two distinct approaches in dealing with the Regulators.

One approach is utilising the asymmetry of information and expertise between the Cheaters and the Regulators, where the Regulators are just persuaded to act in a manner that will benefit the Cheaters. This is the case where the *ability* of the Regulator is inadequate for the proper regulation of the market, although he may not lack the goodwill.

The other approach is to cooperate with the Regulators to share the financial benefits of cheating. This is the case where the *goodwill* of the Regulator is missing, although he may not lack the ability. In other words, this is where corruption enters the picture.

And the best-case for the Cheaters is finding corrupt Regulators without ability. In such cases, extreme benefits can be obtained through sharing only a small portion of the benefit with the corrupt Regulator, as the Regulator will be unaware of the actual scale of the benefit he has created for the Cheaters (and the actual scale of the harm inflicted on the society) and thus will do the job for a relatively small share.

Consequently, the effectiveness of such influence depends on the quality of the human resources that constitute the regulatory bodies. The higher their quality, the more difficult will be to misguide or corrupt them, and thus the lower will be the effectiveness of the cheaters' influence on regulations. A society with adequate Social Intellect, therefore, will try its best to attract the best quality human resources to public service, as will be discussed in Section 6.3.

INFLUENCING LAWMAKING AT MACRO LEVEL

Economy-wide laws and macro-regulations aim to promote the conditions of Fair Competition at the overall economy level, including the protection of the society against cheating on macro-scales and against economy-wide externalities that span many markets.

Consequently, at this macro-level lies the *common corporate interests* of many competitors on the supply side of many different markets. The crucial point here is that, contrary to the case above, several interests of many competitors that compete in totally different markets are common in this macro-economic scale. It directly follows that, such wide groups of competitors with common macro interests span not only the markets where concentrated powers or monopolies exist, but also the markets where close-to-perfect-competition exist.

These common corporate interests usually give birth to several *major concentrated macro-economic interest groups* -and thus major concentrated economic powers- spanning the whole economy.

These concentrated macro-economic interest groups target to influence the Politicians and Lawmakers that direct and regulate the whole economy at the macro-level, and try to misguide them to make laws to their benefit at the expense of the society.

The potential span of such cheating is only limited by imagination, but a few common cases will suffice for illustration:

- To escape the burden of *avoiding or paying for externalities* (the harm given to the society as a result of ongoing operations), some Cheaters misguide Politicians to keep a closed eye on such side-effects – thus cheating directly against the society.

- To maximise their return on capital, some Cheaters (led by the financial institutions, but not limited to them) misguide the Politicians *to weaken the rules for capital adequacy*, which may result in Excessive Risk Taking at the expense of the society – as discussed in Section 3.3.

- To decrease labour costs, many Cheaters try to misguide the Politicians *to dilute labour rights* in general, with excuses like keeping their competitive edge in the global markets - a valid fact but with the wrong remedy.

- To maximise their after-tax profits, many Cheaters misguide the Politicians *to decrease corporate tax rates*, or the Regulators to create sector or market specific tax exemptions, both of which will decrease the tax revenues of the state from corporations and thus necessitate higher taxes on individuals to finance the state budget – thus cheating directly against the society.

- Competitors with concentrated power in their respective markets act in unison *to weaken the anti-trust laws and their practical enforcement* – a case of cheating against all victims simultaneously. Plus, to prevent the entry of new rivals to their sectors, they will lobby for further common advantages, like having stronger intellectual property laws or enforcing non-compete clauses in labour contracts.

- Some Cheaters try to guide the Politicians to *fix or change the conditions of free trade and all the related free flows regarding the opening or closing of their economies to global competition.* The competitors in the markets where the local competitors have a competitive advantage over their global rivals, try to guide the Politicians for ever-more open economies and free trade. On the contrary, the competitors in the markets where the local competitors have a competitive dis-advantage against their global rivals, try to guide the Politicians for closer economies and limited free trade. As the global conditions change over time, the group that dominates the other also changes, and the net pressure on the Politicians shifts from one extreme to the other. In both cases, however, the society ends up being the net loser.

Once again, the effectiveness of the influence of these concentrated macro-economic interest groups on the Politicians and Lawmakers depends on the quality of the human resources that choose to join the political arena. Naturally, the Cheaters would love to see that the Politicians and Lawmakers have minimal ability and goodwill. In contrast, therefore, a society with high Social Intellect should make sure that the Politicians and Lawmakers have maximum ability and goodwill, to handle their job in the best possible manner for the society. But those attributes do not come for free, and the society should realise the necessity to pay for good governance, as will be discussed in Section 6.3.

Naturally, the price of good governance will be in line with the difficulty of the job. And the difficulty of the job, as will be discussed next, is sky-high.

6.2   Regulation And The Optimal Dose

A Matter Of Delicate Balances

In all previous chapters, the significance of proper regulation is emphasized over and over again. This is simply because of *the necessity of optimal regulation for the optimal allocation of resources*, which in turn will maximise the wealth and the welfare of the society in the long run.

To wrap up the previous discussion, proper regulation is required to:

- care for asymmetries of information between producers and consumers
- prevent externalities and promote the best interest of the society
- promote free competition – preferably a fair one
- promote innovation and development
- prevent cheating
- prevent under or over competition – namely monopolies and zombies

One major trouble with regulation is the *lack of regulation* in some markets where it is vital for the elimination of asymmetry of information and externalities. One may tend to think that such cases of missing regulation is a matter of the past, at least in the major markets of our day that have vital importance on the welfare of the society. On the contrary, many high-technology based markets emerged in the recent decades are almost non-regulated, in spite of their tremendous potential impact on the functioning of the western economic and political systems.

The next major trouble with regulation, in markets where it already exists, is *the failure to establish the optimal balance* and having either too little or too much of it. The trouble here stems from the fact that some requirements mentioned above are contradictory in nature in terms of the amount of regulation they necessitate. For instance, to promote free competition, innovation and development, regulations should be kept at low levels. But keeping regulations too low will immediately enable the spread of cheating. Reciprocally, highly regulated markets that fully prevent cheating, will harm free competition and innovation. Therefore, a delicate balance in regulation that will minimise cheating, while still enabling free competition and innovation at a satisfactory level, will be the optimal choice.

Such contradictory requirements make life extremely difficult for the Regulator. In many cases, the Cheaters utilise the excuse that too much regulation harms free competition and innovation, and push for too little regulation that will enable them to cheat easily against the society. This may initially direct the Regulator to under-regulate. But the following spread of cheating in the market eventually causes some sort of market failure, against which the society heavily demands appropriate regulation, and then the Regulator has no choice but to increase the dose of regulation. But in most cases such reactionary regulation ends up in over-regulation, which wipes out any meaningful competition or innovation, and causes another type of market failure sooner or later. This dynamic of oscillating between under and over regulation harms both the market and the society in the long run.

Such oscillating behaviour between under and over regulation is an unfortunate sign of the fact that the Regulators do not exactly know what to regulate or how to regulate. As both under and over regulation are cases of mis-regulation to be avoided, the Regulators should be capable enough (well educated, well experienced and well informed) to determine where the optimal balance lies. And again, that is a matter of quality of human resources – as will be discussed in the next section.

Although attaining optimal regulation is primarily the responsibility of the Regulator, the burden of optimal regulation should also be shared by the society, such that the Regulator should always have and feel the strong support of the society against the Cheaters, to enact the necessary regulations for the optimal balance and fully enforce them. Unfortunately, that was not what has happened in most of the economically advanced western societies in the latest decades.

Tools Of Regulating The Markets

The state need not, and preferably should not, be a player in any market (except in some few cases where it is strategically necessary), but it has to regulate the market such that

- the competitors will play a fair game that will optimize the outcome,

and more importantly,

- the game can not and will not be won at the expense of the best interests of the society.

In trying to achieve that throughout the economy, the Lawmakers and Regulators have two basic set of tools that have to be adjusted to the particular properties of each market: setting the barriers to entry and exit for that market, and defining the limits of freedom and thus the conditions of competition within that market.

BALANCING THE BARRIERS TO ENTRY AND EXIT

Regulation can create barriers to entry and/or barriers to exit for a market. In the simplest terms, barriers to entry make it more difficult for the new competitors to enter the market, thus decreasing the competition within the market, while barriers to exit make it more difficult for the existing competitors to leave the market, thus increasing the competition within the market. To achieve optimal competition within the market, the Regulator has to balance these two barriers delicately.

One option is keeping both the barriers to entry and exit low, such that, while a new competitor can easily come in, a failing one can easily leave too, maximising free competition in the long run. Although this option is the most advertised in the textbooks, in practise it should only be applied under two conditions. First, the investment required to join the market should be relatively low, such that, in case a new competitor fails to calculate its risks properly and faces failure eventually, the final misallocation of resources and hence the damage to the welfare of the society will only be minimal. And second, the exit of any failing competitor should not damage the rest of the market.

Another option is keeping both the barriers to entry and exit high, such that, only the competitors who are qualified and strong enough to stand heavy competition are permitted in the market, as it is undesirable (for the good of the society) for any competitor to leave the market once it is in. In practise, this approach should be preferred in markets where two conditions (both of which are contrary to those above) hold. First, the investment required to join the market is relatively high, and thus, in case a new competitor fails to calculate its risks properly and faces failure eventually, the final misallocation of resources and hence the damage to the welfare of the society will be excessive. And second, the exit of any failing competitor may significantly damage the rest of the market. The finance sector, where the public trust in institutions is a basic requirement, and where any failing player will damage the overall image of the sector, is a classic example.

Barriers to entry can take many forms. Classic barriers include requirements for financial strength and/or sectoral know-how. There are also less recognised ones that may be even more difficult to overcome. One such barrier is the intellectual property rights given to the competitors in a market who have succeeded to make an outstanding innovation. On the one hand, such intellectual property rights are fair rewards and a necessity for ongoing research and development, but on the other hand, they create a significant barrier to entry -at least to a particular portion of the sector- for all other new or existing competitors. While innovation is good for the society, barriers to entry that are kept in place for too long actually harm the interests of the society, as discussed in Section 5.2. A delicate balance by the Regulators is necessary in such cases. Another barrier to entry is the non-compete clauses that are used to limit high-qualified employee transfers to new or existing competitors, practically limiting the circulation of know-how. Again, on the one hand, it is fair for the innovative competitors to try to keep their know-how-developed-in-house inaccessible by their rivals, but on the other hand, limiting technology flow too much for too long slows down the development of the sector and harms the interests of the society in the long run. Another case with a delicate balance requirement for the Regulators.

In many sectors, it is not easy for the Regulator to control the barriers to exit. In such cases, the Regulator is expected to fix the barriers to entry such that an appropriate balance is achieved.

If the barriers to exit are naturally low in a market, and the Regulator rises the barriers to entry, then, while failing competitors easily leave the market, new ones will not be able to come in. The number of existing competitors and therefore the level of competition will continuously decrease, eventually creating an oligopoly or even a monopoly in the market - an undesired outcome as discussed before.

If the barriers to exit are naturally high in a market, and the Regulator lowers the barriers to entry, then, while new competitors can easily and continuously enter the market, failing competitors will not be able to leave that easily and get stuck in the market. The number of existing competitors and the level of competition will continuously increase and profit margins will continuously fall, and eventually an environment of over-competition will be reached where there will be an army of zombies in the market whose profit margins are negative or too low to operate properly. Such an excessive decrease in profit margins, as it is usually coupled with a decrease in prices, will initially be considered as a positive development for the consumer, but, as discussed in Section 5.3, in the long run it will both harm the consumer and decrease the welfare of the society.

SETTING THE OPTIMAL DOSE OF FREEDOM TO COMPETE

Regulation also sets the limits of freedom to compete within a market. On the one hand, it should try to maximise free competition within the market. On the other hand, it should promote fair competition and prevent cheating, in order to protect the competitors, the consumers and the society. Setting such limits of freedom therefore requires a delicate balance that is not easy to achieve in practise.

Taking a closer look, on the one hand, most producers naturally and rightfully demand a wide range of freedoms to let them utilise their competitive advantages and innovative abilities over their rivals in full, which will eventually benefit the consumers and the society as well. On the other hand, Cheaters, hiding behind the Fair Players, push further for freedoms to attain under-regulation, so that they can cheat at the expense of the Fair Players and the consumers and the society. The Regulator is therefore expected to set the rules and limits of competition such that, while the necessary regulations to prevent or at least minimise cheating should be in place, any regulation that unnecessarily limits the freedom to compete should not exist. That is an extremely difficult task to achieve, and many times the balance is wrongfully tilted to one side.

SPREAD OF REGULATORY FAILURE AND REACTIONARY LAWMAKING

If the barriers to entry and exit are not well-balanced, and/or conditions of competition are mis-structured in a particular market, that will create a problem confined to that market. However, in many cases under or over regulation may result from the macro-level economic policies of the Politicians at the Legislative and Executive bodies. In such cases, regulatory failure becomes an economy-wide phenomenon that spans the whole economy[22].

When regulations throughout the whole economy are misbalanced towards any side, such wide-spread failure mostly creates some sort of major economic trouble sooner or later, consequently resulting in a political reaction by the society. In such cases, the extreme-tilt to one side is usually replaced by a reactionary extreme-tilt to the other side, rather than looking for the optimal balance. And than the story will repeat in time, ruining the economic growth and welfare of the society in the long run.

The only way out of this miserable oscillation between the extremes is to have Politicians, Lawmakers and Regulators with adequate ability to start with. But that in turn requires a society with a high Social Intellect to demand and invite such human resources to politics, accepting to pay for it. This will be discussed in Section 6.3, but beforehand, it is crucial to reemphasize the vitality of proper enforcement.

Fair And Complete Enforcement

As discussed in the previous section, escaping the enforcement of laws and regulations is a primary preference for any Cheater, as it creates a competitive advantage against all the rival competitors who can not escape enforcement or willingly choose to compete within the existing regulations. Reading backwards, it is the foremost duty of any Regulator to make sure that all the regulations are fully enforced on all the competitors in a market.

If some Cheaters can behave against regulations while others can not or do not, this will increase the incentives for the Cheaters to do so, as the gap in the competitive advantage to their benefit will be amplified under these conditions. In other words, *partial enforcement of a regulation is much worse than having no regulation at all*, as it ties the hands of the Fair Players while letting the Cheaters cheat freely, enabling them to drive the Fair Players out of the market more easily.

In cases where some Cheaters can escape enforcement, the existence of some regulation, independent of how well designed it may be, does not drive the market towards Fair Competition, but just further away from it. Therefore, *the Regulator must be determined to enforce any regulation fully on each and every competitor, before starting to enact any regulations at all.*

And all this unfortunately means that, Cheaters will try hard to corrupt Regulators to escape enforcement. This clarifies the significance of the goodwill and ethical values of the Regulators, in addition to their ability – as will be discussed in the next section.

6.3   Human Resources In Politics And Bureaucracy

What The Society Needs

The previous chapters and sections revealed that enacting the necessary regulations in an optimal way and enforcing them at all times in all markets on all competitors, prevent cheating and optimise the conditions of competition, consequently maximising the economic development and welfare of the society.

It is important to emphasize that preventing cheating is neither the primary nor the sole target of enacting proper regulations. *In an imaginary society where there are no Cheaters, any mis-regulation resulting from the inability of the Regulators will still cause a misallocation of resources, which in turn will harm the economic development of the society.* Cheating just comes out to be the icing on the cake, as the Cheaters try to misguide the Regulators, or corrupt them whenever misguidance is inapplicable, to tilt the balances to their own benefit.

As discussed above, the making of proper laws and regulations and their flawless enforcement necessitates the existence of high quality human resources in both politics and the bureaucracy. Therefore, *it is in the best interest of the society to have Lawmakers (Politicians) and Regulators (Bureaucrats) who have both professional ability and expertise, and goodwill and ethical values. Unfortunately, these attributes don't come for free - and the Cheaters are well aware of that, even though most societies are not.*

An intellectual society, therefore, should demand to have Politicians and Bureaucrats with utmost ability and goodwill, and be ready to pay for that. And the Cheaters, naturally, do their best to prevent that.

Prevention In Disguise : Irrational Patriotism

Throughout history, and even currently, in almost all societies, patriotism and goodwill are believed to be closely associated with each other, such that, patriotism is considered to be a proxy for the goodwill of a Politician or a Bureaucrat. Unfortunately, at least in practise, it is not.

To overcome this misunderstanding, it is necessary to clarify and distinguish between two concepts: *rational goodwill* versus *irrational patriotism*.

In irrational patriotism, the Politician (or the Bureaucrat) is expected to sacrifice his own being, including his own interests and potential wealth, for the good of the society under all conditions and at all times. Such an unconditional and inescapable sacrifice, unfortunately, does not sound rational to any wise individual in today's societies. It thus follows that, even if there are such patriots, as they most probably fail to satisfy the rationality component, they will lack the necessary ability to succeed in their mission.

In rational goodwill, the Politician (or the Bureaucrat) is expected to serve the society with ability and goodwill, and to sacrifice his own interests if, but only if, necessary, and in return for his qualified service for the best interest of the society and the risk of potential sacrifice he is taking, he has to be both materially compensated and morally honoured.

A society with adequate Social Intellect will redefine patriotism such that it embraces rationality and thus does not contradict with rational goodwill. *Rational patriotism protects both the interests of the society and the interests of the Politician (or Bureaucrat) simultaneously, while placing the interests of the society above that of the Politician (or Bureaucrat) only when they come into conflict.* Becoming a Politician or a Bureaucrat under this scheme will be a rational choice for those who both desire it and are capable of it.

CHEATERS' MISGUIDANCE OF THE SOCIETY

The attraction of Politicians and Bureaucrats with both ability and goodwill to politics and public service, through the scenario where they are compensated fairly in both material and moral terms, will definitely promote the best interests of the society, including its protection against Cheaters.

As a natural consequence, the Cheaters prefer to keep such people away from the political arena by keeping politics and public service to be an unsuitable career for those with superior abilities. And this is most effectively done by promoting irrational patriotism as the foremost attribute of a Politician or a Bureaucrat. And if the Cheaters succeed, the society fails to adequately compensate its Politicians and Bureaucrats materially and morally, and thus drives away all the potential candidates with superior abilities, and leave politics and public service only to those who lack either the ability to serve the society well, or the goodwill to do so, if not both.

To clarify, even if the Politicians or the Bureaucrats are all irrational patriots with the best of intensions for their society and the highest ethical values, their lack of rationality, and thus their lack of superior ability, will still make them incapable of protecting and promoting the interests of the society against those of the Cheaters. The other option, happily made available to the society by the Cheaters, is to elect Politicians or Bureaucrats with superior ability, but without any sincere goodwill and ethical values, so that even though the society will not compensate them properly and fairly, they will create other ways to compensate themselves, most probably cooperating with the Cheaters at the expense of the society.

Unfortunately, *societies with inadequate Social Intellect always fall into this trap, by accepting and demanding irrational patriotism as an undisputable precondition for being a Politician or a Bureaucrat, and not bothering to pay fairly for their expected service, thus condemning themselves to perpetually losing against the Cheaters, by electing either the incapables or the ill-willed to politics and public service.*

Reversing The Intra-Society Brain Drain

Any rational and bright individual who has spent many years of his lifetime educating himself and thus paved his way for a successful career, will naturally aim to create value for the society and get compensated fairly in return, both materially and morally, in a sustainable fashion. And under the current conditions in most societies, such a career expectation, unfortunately, does not cover politics or public service as an alternative, as discussed above.

As a result, for many decades, *societies are experiencing an intra-society brain drain where their best educated and brightest minds are attracted by their private sector, rather than by their public sector, thus preventing the formation of a better Legislation, Execution and bureaucracy that will serve the best interests of these societies.*

To overcome this damaging practise, *any society with adequate Social Intellect should make sure that politics or public service will be a reliable and rational career for such people with both outstanding abilities and goodwill, including satisfying their moral and material needs as good as the other options outside politics or the state.*

A CLOSER LOOK AT MATERIAL COMPENSATION

Allocating a larger portion of the state budget to the compensation of Politicians and Bureaucrats, especially those at the decision-making higher ranks, will actually be a great use of public resources, as more capable and good-willed Politicians and Bureaucrats will generate tremendous value for the society in two separate ways. First, *by maximising the value created for the society through much better political management, lawmaking and regulations.* Second, *by minimizing cheating* and thus minimising the harm inflicted on the society by the Cheaters. And the combination of these two will maximise the economic growth, wealth and welfare of the society in the long run.

STILL TRAPPED INSIDE THE FALLACY

As any society advances its Social Intellect, it should realize the significance and the necessity of maximising the quality of human resources attracted to politics and public service, especially at the decision-making higher ranks. Unfortunately, most societies are still misguided by the Cheaters, and insist on keeping the material compensation of all their Politicians and Bureaucrats at minimal levels, naively believing that they are already heavily rewarded with the honour of sacrificing themselves for the society. And they go on paying for that grave mistake through a tremendous loss of potential wealth and welfare.

Chapter 7

COMPETITION AND CHEATING IN POLITICS

7.1   Competition In Politics

Lack Of Competition In Politics

The basic facts and arguments given for economics in the previous chapters actually apply to politics equally well. And the applications are quite trivial, once it is observed that the Politicians compete like the producers do in economics, supplying services spanning Legislation and Execution, and the voters act like the consumers who search for the best fit for their preferences and try to maximise the value they get out of their choices.

The first and foremost application of economic concepts to politics is that, *competition in politics is equally significant and necessary for the best interest of the society and for maximising its long-term welfare.*

And unfortunately, the major trouble with politics is that, even though competition exists up to some extent in the economies of the western societies, it is next to non-existent in politics in practise. This may be difficult to realize at first sight, as in principle there are two or more political parties in every democratic system and the voters are free to make a choice.

It may be easier to see why competition does not practically exist in politics once a simple analogy is drawn with economics: a product is subject to competition if and only if there is at least one other product, and preferably many other products, that may serve the particular preference of the consumer equally well and thus can replace it. The mere existence of other products which will not fit the preference of the consumer in any way, do not create any competition for a product. In other words, competition requires the existence of rival products that can replace each other. The mere existence of many irrelevant products does not bring any competition to any of them.

From a political viewpoint, this means that *the existence of a few political parties that differentiate themselves based on fundamental differences on some very major issues, such that most of their voters will never consider voting for any other party independent of their performance in general, does not bring much competition to politics.*

These fundamental differences between political parties may be based on economic issues (such as promoting liberal policies versus social policies) or social issues (such as nationality, culture, race, religion etc.) or a combination of the two, but in all cases fundamental differences on major issues will weaken the competition between political parties, as one is not considered to be a potential replacement for the other for very many of their respective voters.

Contrary to common opinion, such irreconcilable differences are not necessarily based on the representation of the two extremes on a major issue by two political parties. In most cases, one party at one extreme is considered to be far away from another one at a moderate standing. For instance, if one party promotes and over-values some social identity while the other party just rejects the importance or value of that identity, rather than promoting the opposite identity, the difference in between is still prohibitive for most voters in terms of switching from one to the other.

In that regard, a political system may even have three outstanding parties differentiating and distancing themselves from each other on one or more major issues, such that two stand at the two opposite extremes and one on a moderate position, and still have inadequate competition. Real competition in politics is more difficult to achieve than initially imagined.

In all cases where there is inadequate competition in politics, the Execution and Legislation still change hands from one party to the other once in a while. Unfortunately, this is not a proof of the existence of a real competition, as the voters who shift from one party to the other are those who do not feel to be closely represented by any of these political parties, and thus who do not much care about the major issues either party focuses on, but base their decisions on other issues on the current political agenda. This practically means that, these voters just vote for these existing parties out of lack of other options. Both the lack of real competition and the resulting frustration of many voters in failing to find a party that really represents their opinions are significant troubles that may undermine the sustainability of the democratic system in the long run.

The necessary structural improvements to introduce real competition in politics and to satisfy the sophisticated voters of our day will be discussed in Book Four, but still the lack of competition in politics and its negative consequences deserve a closer look within the ongoing discussion of this book.

POLITICAL PARTIES MAY NOT WORRY MUCH ABOUT PERFORMANCE

When and where there is little competition between the political parties, each party is practically a monopoly for its loyal voters. And just like in economics, once a competitor reaches monopoly status, it will not really worry about maximising its performance anymore as the consumers (read: voters) have no other choice but its service.

In the economics jargon, for every competitor in every competition, there is a carrot (the benefit he gets in case of success) and a stick (the punishment he faces in case of failure). Applying to politics, in the case where there is little competition, both the carrot and the stick are missing. The stick is missing, because even if these political parties do not perform well, they will not be losing many votes of their supporters based on their weak performance. The carrot is also missing, because even if these political parties perform well, they will not be getting many additional votes of their opposers for their high performance. Therefore, *in cases where real competition is missing, the political parties have limited motivation to try harder to improve their performance, as their performance have only a marginal effect on the votes they will get in the next election.*

BEST INTEREST OF THE SOCIETY MAY NOT BE SERVED

When the competition in politics is on major issues only, all the non-major issues may easily get neglected. This is the equivalent of our observation in economics in Section 4.2 that, any attribute (read: non-major issue) that is not observed or cared about by the consumer (read: voter) will end up at the worst quality. Similarly, in politics, *when voters base their decisions on a few major issues only, the non-major issues may be neglected, or worse, may not be handled at the best interest of the society, but rather to the benefit of some other concentrated interest groups at the expense of the society.*

POLITICAL PARTIES SHIFTING TO EXTREMES

As discussed in Section 5.4, in economics, when there is under-competition (resulting from the existence of a monopoly) somewhere, it creates over-competition somewhere else. The same is valid in politics too, albeit with a worse outcome.

When there is under-competition *between* the political parties, there is over-competition *within* the political parties, as the candidates for outstanding positions in each party have to somehow distinguish themselves from the rest of their rivals who share relatively similar opinions on the major issues defended by their party. The lack of other similar political parties to which the candidates aspiring for top level political jobs (including the party leadership) can go, makes it necessary to win the competition within that single party. And in practise, this results in the candidates' shifting to more extreme political opinions to differentiate themselves in the in-party competition. Consequently, each party gets dominated by the extremists inside it, driving the rival parties further away from each other.

This phenomenon (of the over-competition within each political party driving the candidates and the parties towards more extreme political opinions) is supported by two other significant developments. The first is the deterioration of the economic and social conditions during the latest decades, and the rise of economic inequality within the societies, fuelling an anger in the society against the current policies and Politicians. The second is the falling Social Intellect of the societies (as discussed in Book One) that prevents the correct diagnosis of the reasons and the cures of these developments, making the societies vulnerable to populist approaches that usually embrace extremism.

A GLIMPSE OF THE REMEDY FOR LACK OF COMPETITION

The long-term remedy to this dangerous shift to extremism on each side of the political spectrum is increasing the competition between the political parties within the democratic system. This requires the emergence of many political parties in the political competition such that these parties may have a real chance to change the end result of the elections. But, in economic terms, such a rise in production (i.e. in the number of political parties) will require an increase on both the demand and the supply sides. Applying to politics, the demand for new political parties can only follow a rise in the Social Intellect of the society. And a rise in the supply of new Politicians and new political parties necessitate significant changes in the rules of the game within the democratic system such that the newcomers to politics may have an expectation of some potential success. All these will be discussed in detail in Book Four of this series.

The Rise Of Populism

THE EMERGENCE OF CONVENIENT CONDITIONS FOR POPULISM

By the end of the 20th century, the wealth of many economically advanced western societies have risen to very high levels relative to the rest of the world. The economic and political conditions, however, were getting more and more cloudy, both inside and outside.

Within these western societies, the too liberal economic policies of the previous decades have risen the concentration of economic power and decreased competition in both goods/services and labour markets, creating a chain of reactions that eventually increased economic inequality, which in turn started to harm the welfare[23] of these societies. Technological advancements enabled more and more automation in production lines, increasing efficiency on the one hand, but decreasing the demand for less-qualified labour on the other, transferring wealth from labour to capital. Many major corporations in the western societies have lobbied their governments for more economic globalisation solely considering their own benefit, and got what they wanted. As a result of this mis-structured economic globalisation, which will be discussed in another book of this series, they became global corporations and skyrocketed their fortunes. However, reaching new markets and new consumers was just one of the reasons behind the rise of their fortunes. Another equally significant reason was the access to the cheap labour, which practically meant transferring wealth from the less qualified labour in their own societies to the labour in the developing societies. This resulted in a very uneven distribution of the benefits of globalisation, where the main loser was the less qualified labour in the western societies. Free trade and the resulting trade imbalances (to the benefit of the developing societies of the east) further fuelled the flow of wealth from the western societies to the developing ones in the east. The emerging trade surpluses to the benefit of the other societies were channelled back to the financial markets of the western societies and financed the borrowing-based consumption in the western societies, and that enabled the rising income inequality within the western societies to stay unnoticed for a long time, until the indebtedness of the consumers reached unsustainable levels.

And all these simultaneous major changes in the environment and the rising complexity resulting from them, has caused *a weakening of Social Intellect* in the western societies, which has proceeded in the dark for decades. This has prevented the realisation of what has really been going on around by the masses, and the music played until all blew up in 2008.

To cut the long story short, all the structural problems within and between the societies that have been accumulating for decades, have surfaced within a short period of time in such a way that they have created a perfect storm.

For each society, such an outburst of accumulated major structural problems necessitates changes not only in its macro-policies and strategies, but also in the main structure of its economic and political systems. And implementing such a major change will require a re-balancing of the society's short-term versus long-term interests, with the long-term taking priority, such that the short-term sacrifices the society has to make to protect its long-term interests (and welfare) are now much higher than ever before. This is a fact that is extremely difficult for any society to accept, especially while its Social Intellect is weakening.

When these societies have faced a decrease in welfare, accompanied by a realisation of the heavy burden they have incurred, they have naturally blamed their current Politicians and their economic policies. This verdict was partially fair, as their current Politicians' ability and goodwill had significant deficiencies. And it was partially unfair, because, if these societies had not been losing Social Intellect for decades, they would not have passively watched the accumulation of all these structural problems in the first place and would have already demanded significant economic and social policy changes before the storm.

And unfortunately, the surfacing of the accumulated structural problems in both economics and politics over the latest decades, as a result of political mismanagement coupled with the weakening of the Social Intellect of the societies, have eventually created a perfect breeding ground for the populists.

THE POPULISTS

As discussed in detail in Book One of this series, any social issue that needs deep analysis and painful long-term solutions, which makes it difficult to understand and painful to accept, is a candidate for the populist politician to feed on through misconceptions, wrong and shallow analysis, and irrational short-term solutions. And the more the society loses its Social Intellect, the easier it gets for the populist politician to misguide and persuade many voters. Thus came the rise of populism in the recent decades: very many accumulated structural troubles simultaneously surfacing on the one hand, society losing intellect further on the other.

And when the ground is ready for populism, the extremists in all political parties who have already been gaining power within their parties, embrace populism - as selling extremist messages with simple and straightforward sentences is very convenient.

INEVITABLE FAILURE OF POPULIST POLICIES

It may be argued that, a populist's coming to power may not be a long-term problem in a Democracy: even if a populist politician manages to win an election, once in power he will start to fail immediately. He either can not apply the promised policies since they are inapplicable in practise anyway, or applies some of them and the voters will then experience the negative results. Both ways will lead to a loss for him in the next election, and thus the problem will solve itself.

There may be a bit of truth in this. However, even if this will be the case, a severe damage will already be done by the time the populist leaves power. This is simply because *the populist not only worsens the existing problems by not treating them, but also adds new problems to the agenda by his wrong policies.* And this will steal decades from the future of the society and from the lives of the coming generations, even if rational politicians are elected to power immediately afterwards.

There is also the possibility that the society will try a few populists one after the other before realizing the need for rational policies, and unfortunately, in such cases the social order of the society may get seriously harmed in the meantime.

POLITICIANS DESPERATELY REVERTING TO POPULISM

Applying basic concepts of economics to politics, it can be said that economic and social policies are the products of a Politician that he aims to sell to the society and get paid in return by receiving their votes. In this regard, any political opinion has to be marketable to the society in order to attract votes.

A marketable opinion, in turn, has to have two attributes. First, it should be understandable with respect to the adequacy of the Social Intellect of the society. And second, it should be likeable if and when understood.

Unfortunately, in the complex environment of our day, the remedies for the current structural troubles in economics and politics also need to be complex. Moreover, they mostly require short-term sacrifices for long-term benefits. Therefore, they are neither easily understandable nor much likeable, and fail to satisfy both of the above conditions.

In light of this unfortunate fact, if a Politician insists on giving the right messages and making the right promises, which means presenting the complex, painful but correct long-term solutions, he simply can not get sufficient support to win an election and apply his policies.

Consequently, Politicians have no choice but to change and simplify their political opinions and promises on policies such that they become understandable and likeable. However, such changes and simplifications mostly make their policies inadequate, and at many cases plain wrong. The trouble here is that, *many Politicians who are actually capable, sincere and ethical, are forced by the inadequacy of the Social Intellect of the society to generate populist solutions.*

And *even worse, many potential Politicians who are not willing to do so, but see no other way to succeed in politics due to the inadequacy of the Social Intellect of the society, simply stay away from politics, at the expense of the society.*

As was discussed in Book One and will be discussed again in Book Four of this series, *in a Democracy no one can save the society unless the society develops adequate Social Intellect to demand to be saved by rational policies instead of following populist promises.*

7.2 Cheating In Politics

Cheaters In Politics

Just like in economics, there will always be some potential Cheaters in politics trying to serve their own political interests at the expense of the rest. Some of these may revert to cheating simply because they are not merited enough to succeed without cheating. Others may be too greedy to be satisfied by any success achievable through a fair play in politics. And finally, some may just believe that, even though they may have some merit and achieved some success in politics, their current success is more of a result of their own good luck or the bad luck of their rivals, and the winds may someday turn to reverse their fortunes, and thus they need to cheat to sustain their success.

These Cheaters act recklessly to harm both the political system and the welfare of the society to serve their own benefits, and in doing so, they may utilise any approach that may come to mind. Among all those approaches utilised by these Cheaters, the ones discussed in the rest of this section are less recognised by the society, but inflict the greatest harm to its welfare. Their conceptual similarity with the cheating approaches in economics discussed in the previous chapters will be self-evident.

The Prerequisite For Cheating In Politics : Inadequacy Of Social Intellect

The inadequacy of the Social Intellect of the society is a prerequisite for cheating in both economics and politics, but with a fundamental difference in between.

In economics there are so many different markets that, independent of the level of his Social Intellect, a consumer can not focus on all the individual markets and minimise the asymmetry of information between himself and the producers. For that reason, there has to be a wide set of laws and regulations to protect and promote the interests of the consumer.

In politics, however, there is no such dispersion of attention, and thus, in case his Social Intellect is adequate, the voter can focus on the developments and minimise the asymmetry of information between himself and the Politicians. This makes a rise in the Social Intellect of the society a more immediate and significant obstacle for the Cheaters in politics. And consequently, the cheating Politicians try their best to keep Social Intellect of the society as low as possible as long as possible, so that they can cheat as much as possible.

And unfortunately, the lower the Social Intellect of the society falls, the higher will be its tendency to stay that way, simply because the less the society will be aware of its own intellectual weakness and the less it will demand a cure.

SOCIAL INTELLECT, REVISITED

Social Intellect is the combination of social education and social awareness.

Social education, in turn, can be acquired either through a formal education or through informal communication. The path through formal education is definitely much faster and much better, and for that reason, it was proposed in Book One that a society should supply a mandatory social education for all its citizens at their early years of adulthood (or later for those who have missed that chance), if they are expected to act as rational voters throughout the rest of their lives. And again exactly for that reason, Cheaters in politics decisively neglect any such need and are determined to keep the current practise in education -which may rise any sort of professional expertise but not Social Intellect- intact. Fortunately, the spread of digital communication networks enables the dispersion of arguments on social issues, and through such channels of informal communication, at least some members of the society -who may have some slight interest in economics and politics- have a chance to develop their knowledge on relevant issues. This is much slower and less efficient for sure, but works persistently to serve the purpose.

The second condition for having adequate Social Intellect is spending time and effort to keep social awareness. And that requires having access to complete and correct information on the developments in economics and politics, preferably by the individual himself, or in cases where that is not easy, at least by the genuine experts who will then share their opinion with the individual.

And exactly for that reason, the Cheaters in politics try their best to maximise the asymmetry of information between themselves and the rest of the society.

Cheating Through Asymmetry Of Information

Cheaters have many classic ways to prevent the free flow of complete and correct information. One approach is censoring out vital information, and whenever this is not possible, crowding out vital information with too much noise or additional irrelevant information such that the information required for rational decision making can not be filtered out easily or quickly.

In cases where the access to information can not be prevented effectively, another approach is *trying to decrease the demand for information, by distracting the attention of the voters away from social issues.* One way of doing this is directing the attention of the society to the infinitely many sorts of entertainment. With the help of the mind-blowing developments in digital technologies (enabling endless free flow of shows and videos, internet games, social media…) this last option is gaining tremendous effectiveness in serving the purposes of the Cheaters -as will be discussed in the next sub-section-, but there are also other classic approaches that never diminish in effectiveness.

PERCEPTION MANAGEMENT

In principle, Politicians are expected to focus on the issues of critical importance for the society and explain why their policies on those issues are superior to their rivals' and thus how they will further increase the welfare of the society if they get elected. However, *in practise, Politicians try to focus the society's attention to issues in which they believe they have an edge against their rivals or their rivals have relative weaknesses, even though those issues may not be the most critical ones for the welfare of the society under the prevailing conditions at that specific time. Similarly, they may try to shift focus away from the issues of critical importance for the society, if they believe they have a weakness there or their rivals have some relative strength.*

While carrying out such perception management, the Cheaters present correct but incomplete or irrelevant information, and in that regard such behaviour is not illegal, or even only marginally unethical as long as no lies are involved. But it shifts attention from the critical issues and misguides the society. Unfortunately, *the weaker the society's Social Intellect gets, the easier the Cheaters will divert the discussion away from the issues of real importance towards irrelevant or less important ones.*

HIDING THE BEST OPTION

Another approach frequently used by the Cheaters is presenting only two options, such that one option serves their own purposes while the other option is a totally unacceptable one, thus leaving their desired option as the only practical choice. This requires *hiding the moderate options as if they don't exist and presenting only two opposing extremes, such that, on one extreme they stand themselves and the other extreme is even worse and thus totally unacceptable.* The moderate options, which will dominate both extremes if presented, are carefully hidden and left out of discussion.

For instance, in many cases in history, *societies were presented the two extreme options for their economic systems, the hard-core-socialism versus wild-capitalism, while the best option, a Free Market Economy with proper regulation and fair competition, was hidden with utmost care.*

As the society increases its Social Intellect, it realizes that there are almost always balanced options which dominate the extremes and demands to be presented those as well – with all the shades of grey between the two extremes. And the higher the Social Intellect of the society gets, the higher will be its chance to find out the optimal grey option.

Reading backwards, if the Social Intellect of the society starts to weaken, as has been happening in the recent decades, the options at the extremes mostly presented through some touch of populism, will start to emerge as possible remedies to the society's troubles while the moderate paths will fall out of attention.

Cheating Utilising High-Tech

The emergence of digital technologies in the latest decades have paved the way for the creation of very effective cheating tools that can be expected to spread exponentially in the foreseeable future, with the potential harm to the western social order rising in similar magnitudes in due course.

To make matters much worse, the supply of these technologies and the products based on them are in the hands of a few high-tech monopolies, with two dangerous consequences for the society. First, as will be explained below, having monopoly status on information flow increases the potential effectiveness of these technologies in cheating. Second, these monopolies pose a risk of -wilful or forced- cooperation with the Cheaters in politics to manipulate the society to serve their own interests.

The potential success in manipulation of opinions depends both on the level of the Social Intellect of the society and the effectiveness of the manipulation techniques, both of which are changing over time. When the manipulation techniques offered by digital technologies are developing at a mind-blowing speed while the Social Intellect of the societies are weakening, democracies are undeniably in grave danger.

CONTROLLING INFORMATION FLOW AND MANIPULATING OPINIONS

High-tech monopolies not only have access to all the personal information on their users, but they also track the digital footprint of each individual very closely and continuously on a personal basis, including their economic and political preferences and behaviour. This infinite access to such personal information enables these monopolies to know their users even better than the users know themselves. And as they are monopolies in their respective fields, they gather information on all the members of the society, leaving no one out. Then, the analysis of this society-wide information by advanced big-data algorithms enables the accurate prediction of the potential reactions of both the individuals and the society under various conditions and circumstances.

High-tech monopolies also control the flow of data to their users. They may direct the information flow to serve the interests of some concentrated interest groups they may be cooperating with. They can make sure that any information against their interests does not reach either to the individual or to the society, while any information -real or fabricated- that suits their own interests surely does.

Preventing the spread of information against their interests can be done in many ways. One way is controlling the search engines that will do the censorship for them without being known by the society. They can potentially wipe out any person, any corporate or political entity, or any idea that they don't want their users to get informed on. Another way, which is more effective, is to crowd out the environment with too much noise such that any undesired information will not be noticed by the society. And thanks to the recent developments in artificial intelligence, creating noise on a grand scale is now much simpler.

Spreading real information that suits their own interests is trivial. But the most effective method is spreading fake or fabricated information, which can be used either to benefit themselves or to harm others.

The latest developments in artificial intelligence enable the fabrication of fake photos, videos, stories, news and all other sorts of digital material easier than ever before. Such fake material can already be easily produced for society-wide distribution, but the effectiveness of such material is limited for two reasons. First, any material that is produced in a one-size-fits-all fashion will have a marginal effect on each individual. And second, any counter parties that may be harmed by such material (say political rivals) will immediately respond in one way or another, to reverse the effect of such action.

The real effective tool will therefore be the tailor-made fabrication and communication of fake material on an individual basis – which is the next stage on horizon. As each individual's digital footprint reveals his personal background, beliefs, preferences, tendencies, desires, fears and especially intellectual weaknesses, such personal production of fake material will have maximum effect on shaping his perception and opinion. Moreover, nobody else will know that he is exposed to such fake material and thus no one can respond to eliminate or dilute the effect of such individually communicated material.

In short, when the capability to have personal information and analysis for each individual in the society, combines with the capability to control information flow on an individual basis, the manipulation of the opinion and the perception of any individual may be possible. And the successful manipulation of -not necessarily all but- most of the individuals will practically result in the manipulation of the society.

It is time for every society to realize that any monopolies or any concentration of power in the digital environment, enabling information gathering, analysis, fabrication and flow on a society-wide scale is too dangerous and can potentially harm the interests of the society and even the stability of its social order. The failure of both the Regulators and the societies in the recent past in recognizing these potential dangers of the existence of such monopolies, has significantly increased the cost of dealing with these monopolies today. Considering the potential negative consequences, however, the societies should be willing to pay the high price to break up such monopolies and/or enact the necessary regulations before it is too late.

DISTRACTING ATTENTION TO DIMINISH SOCIAL AWARENESS

Social awareness is the greatest obstacle to cheating, especially in politics. For that reason, distraction of attention from social issues to any sort of entertainment makes cheating much easier. In that regard, the ongoing developments in digital technologies that offer new and sophisticated tools of entertainment are innocent but effective assistants for the Cheaters.

The next revolutionary development in digital entertainment will be virtual reality, which is primarily a complete immersion of the individual to artificial worlds created for the tastes of the individual by the individual with the help of artificial intellect. For that purpose, new sets of gizmos will be utilized, enabling the total isolation of the individual from his environment, and letting him to hear or see only the artificial world created around him. As this imaginary world is tailor-made to maximise his pleasure, with the help of artificial intelligence that knows the individual better than he knows himself, the individual will feel like he is in a heaven on earth whenever he is submerged in this artificial world. Staying in such an imaginary world for extended periods of time in a frequent fashion will weaken his ties with the realities of the world he is living in. This will both diminish his motivation, and steal the time and effort he needs, to stay aware of his economic and political environment, diluting his social awareness of the real world he is living in – to the very pleasure of the Cheaters.

To make matters worse, in his artificial heaven on earth, the individual will be completely free to do whatever he wants and to live in any way he desires, downgrading the importance any potential loss of freedom he may experience in the real world due to the deterioration of his social environment. Similarly, he can be infinitely happy in his artificial world, and may not care about his lack of happiness in this world based on any rising inequality against him or the decrease in his welfare.

In short, he may easily lose his Social Intellect, becoming an easy-to-guide prey for the Cheaters, without any motivation to act in any manner to improve -or even protect- his own welfare and thus that of the society. He may not question any social issues and may not show any political reaction to promote his interests through the democratic system, making life exponentially easier for the Cheaters.

Needless to say, there may be other technological developments that can not be imagined today, but will be even more effective on distracting the attention of the intellectually inadequate members of the society, so both the time and the trend are on the Cheaters' side. The society, therefore, has to act fast enough to increase the Social Intellect of most of its members to adequate levels, such that they will not fall into such traps posed by any potential distractors of attention.

Cheating Through Excessive Long-Term Borrowing

Overly-expansionary fiscal policies give a boost to the performance of all Politicians under most conditions, as they fuel the growth of the economy. Although they usually have negative side effects (like inflation) in the medium run, they are extremely convenient for short-term cheating purposes, like winning an election in the near future. All that is needed are financing these policies without creating an immediate economic burden on the voters, and a society with an inadequate Social Intellect to be impressed by such policies.

As additional taxes on the current voters do not fulfil the condition above, the most convenient financing for this purpose is long-term borrowing in excessive amounts. However, such long-term borrowing creates a heavy tax burden for the future generations, as somebody has to pay back that debt someday in the future.

The future generations, who are not yet born or are too young to vote in the current elections, are not represented in today's political system, and have no political power to defend their rights. For that reason, promoting the interest of the existing generation at the expense of these future generations through excessive long-term borrowing, is equivalent to cheating against the future generations. In principle, such cheating should be morally unacceptable in a society with adequate Social Intellect. But, unfortunately, that is not the case in practise in most societies, and many cheating Politicians get away with such policies and may end up winning the coming elections. And this makes the voters of such Politicians partners in cheating with them, as passively keeping a closed eye on such policies can not be an excuse for anybody.

Cheating Through Excessive Risk Taking

Sometimes the performance of the Politicians on duty is undeniably weak. In such cases, even they realize themselves that they do not stand much of a chance to win the next election. They may then start to look for a performance booster in their time left until the end of the current term, accepting all the excessive risks associated with it, as they have nothing left to lose.

Just like in economics, deliberate excessive risk taking in politics is taking an unnecessary extremely risky action where any potential profits (like winning the next election) will be kept by the Politicians in case of success, while any potential losses in case of failure will be borne by the society.

In politics excessive risks can be taken in many ways, spanning economics, domestic politics and international relations. One classic way of taking such excessive risks in the economic front is heavy borrowing followed by public spending in the short-term to make voters temporarily happy until the elections and worry about the medium-term consequences later – as discussed in the previous sub-section. On the political front, a common approach is promoting extremist ideas to diminish the attention to the real issues of failure until the elections, only to worry about the consequences afterwards. On the international relations front, leaving alliances (like the European Union or NATO) or rising military tensions with other societies are common.

Again, just like in economics, all such unnecessary excessive risk taking behaviour at the expense of the society is equivalent to cheating against the society. Moreover, when such excessive risks are taken, the coming generations who are not even represented in politics today, may have to share and pay the price as well, spreading the scope of such cheating to the future generations.

Unlike in economics, it difficult to quantify the positive or negative values of possible outcomes of excessive risk taking in politics. However, one basic concept in economics, namely the risk taking capacity mentioned in Section 3.2, can still be adopted to politics. The society can take into consideration the worst possible outcome of a political action, and evaluate whether it can survive or would like to bear its consequences in the medium to long-term. *A society with adequate Social Intellect should never reward any Politician for taking unnecessary excessive-risks with potential catastrophic consequences, but just on the contrary should punish him in the elections for doing so, even if the imagined potential positive outcome of such risks may be very tempting.* Unfortunately, in the intellectually inadequate societies just the opposite is happening, motivating the Politicians for further cheating through excessive risk taking.

7.3   Concentration Of Power In Politics

Emergence Of Concentration Of Power In Politics

Just like in economics, success may come through a blend of merit or luck or cheating in politics. And in practise, an outstanding success in politics rarely comes as a result of cheating alone, unless merit or luck initially accompanies it.

In politics, therefore, initial outstanding success mostly arise out of a stellar performance in either the economic or the political fronts.

In principle, outstanding success in the economic front may come as a result of pursuing new or different policies that result in a significant rise in the wealth and welfare of the society in the short to medium terms. In practise, it usually comes as a result of inheriting an economy that was initially in a disastrous condition, thanks to the inability of the previous Politicians, or some extremely negative external conditions beyond their control, or just bad luck. Starting from such a low reference point, either the barely rational moves by the new Politicians on duty, or the self-correction of external conditions, or the reversal of bad luck, will result in significant positive developments in the economic front. And any society with inadequate Social Intellect will naively assume such success to be the result of the new policies, over-appreciating the Politicians currently on duty. And this is a golden opportunity for the Politicians to over-accumulate the political support of the society, which in turn enables them to concentrate their political power without much opposition.

On the political front, there may be similar instances of non-economic nature. In principle, creating or joining an international alliance to better protect the society, or attaining a dominant position in the global arena, or winning an ongoing war, can all be reasons for achieving outstanding success. In practice, luck may still intervene. For instance, the disintegration or failure of a major international rival or alliance, mostly resulting from their internal weaknesses or structural troubles that have been accumulating for decades, may seem to be the success of the current Politicians and policies. In a well known recent case, the collapse of the Soviet Alliance was taken to be the success of the western social order, giving too much undeserved credit to the extremely liberal policies that have eventually resulted in the 2008 crisis.

In any case, a major economic or political success will bring undisputed political credit to the Politicians on duty, practically creating a temporary concentration of political power. But again, no success is eternal if competition exists and survives.

Just like in economics, in a competitive political environment, such power will weaken over time as memories of the current success fade and other new troubles inevitably emerge in either economics or politics. And therefore, even if political power is initially attained through success based on merit or luck rather than cheating, keeping and strengthening political power in the long run requires the weakening of competition. And then comes the natural urge for cheating, even in the cases where it was absent before.

Cooperation Of Economic And Political Powers

CONCENTRATED MACRO-ECONOMIC INTEREST GROUPS, REVISITED

As discussed in Section 6.1, many kinds of corporate interests of many competitors on the supply side of many different markets are common on the macro-economic scale. Consequently, many of these competitors constitute concentrated macro-economic interest groups -and thus concentrated economic powers spanning the whole economy- that usually act in unison to extract macro-benefits for themselves.

To promote their own interests, these concentrated macro-economic interest groups will need to lobby on and misguide the Politicians to make laws to their benefit at the expense of the society. Alternatively, they -or some of their members- may look for Cheaters in politics with whom they may cooperate to serve their mutual interests, without the need to lobby to misguide them.

And *in practise, either of these aims can be achieved much more easily and effectively in case there is a concentrated political power to deal with.* Consequently, concentrated macro-economic interest groups -or some of their members- may support the creation and/or continuation of such concentrated political power.

COOPERATION OF CONCENTRATED ECONOMIC AND POLITICAL POWERS

If it were only these concentrated macro-economic interest groups seeking the cooperation of a concentrated political power, their search may have ended in vain. But unfortunately, such search for cooperation exists on both sides.

If and when some concentrated political power somehow emerges, it will need to cooperate with economic powers to reach the financial resources that will enable the continuation of its political interests in the long run. And for that reason, both the concentrated macro-economic interest groups and the concentrated political power may easily find reliable partners in each other.

Any potential cooperation between the two will then span the whole spectrum from economics to politics. And as they support and strengthen each other through such cooperation, they start to inflict a heavier harm on the welfare of the society.

THE MISERY OF THE SOCIETY

The welfare of the society is not solely based on the total wealth of the society, but also on the distribution of that wealth within the society, namely inequality - as will be discussed in detail in Book Three of this series.

While the cooperating economic and political powers pursue their own interests at the expense of the society, the welfare of the society starts to fall at an ever increasing speed, due to the deterioration in both of these fronts.

The economic growth and development of the society will slow down, or may even turn to negative, as the cheating of the economic and political powers will cause a misallocation of resources to their own benefit.

To keep its cooperation alive with its partners in cheating, the concentrated political power has to sustain and further rise the benefits of the concentrated economic powers in time, even though the growth rate of the economy may slow down or turn to negative. This will cause the share of the cooperating concentrated powers within the overall economy to rise further, while, consequently, the share of the rest of the society will fall. And this will result in an excessive rise in the inequality within the society.

When economic growth rate slows down or falls to negative, while the inequality within the society reaches excessive levels, the welfare of the society falls tremendously. In simpler words, as the total size of the cake and the share of the rest of the society within the cake decreases simultaneously, the society becomes terribly unhappy.

THE REMEDY

The prevention of the cooperation of concentrated economic and political powers is necessary for the well functioning of the western social order based on Free Market Economy and Democracy.

In the societies with adequate Social Intellect, not only the concentrations of power in the micro-scale (in the individual markets) are prevented, but also the influence of the concentrated macro-economic interest groups on politics is weakened -or even nullified- by the solid political demand of the society through democratic means.

Unfortunately, in practise, even if a society starts from a high enough intellectual level, the sustainability of the adequacy of its Social Intellect can not always be guaranteed. Simultaneous occurrence and overlapping of major developments may cause a sudden weakening of the Social Intellect of the society from time to time and result in a fall below the necessary threshold. In such cases, first, concentrations of power or monopolies in the micro-scale emerge, and second, the influence of the concentrated macro-economic interest groups strengthen at the expense of the interests of the society.

However, *even if such concentrated economic powers emerge and/or strengthen in the markets and/or in the economy, they can still be properly dealt with (prevented on the micro-scale and weakened on the macro-scale), as long as there is no concentrated political power to cooperate with them. In* other words, *all troubles regarding the concentration of powers in the economy can be handled without any significant long-term harm to the society, as long as politics (Democracy) functions well, as politics has decisive control over the economic system.*

And therefore, *the prevention of the concentration of power in politics comes out to be a necessary condition for the well functioning of the western social order.*

Natural Destruction Of Concentrated Political Power

Any concentrated political power may sometime face a catastrophic failure that will abruptly end its grip on power. A heavy economic crisis that wipes out the purchasing power of most members of the society or a war lost with heavy casualties are common instances. And sometimes bad luck intervenes. External developments beyond its control, like a global economic crisis or a global pandemic, may reverse its fortunes. In any case no political power is invincible or eternal, and will be lost someday somehow.

However, that does not mean that a functioning Democracy can be restored in any such way.

First, such an economic or political crisis has to be so sudden and catastrophic that the concentrated political power will be caught off-guard and fail to protect itself. But this practically means that the emergence of such a crisis may take a long time, during which the social order and the welfare of the society will suffer a heavy damage, and worse, the Social Intellect of the society may weaken beyond the minimum threshold to revive the social order.

And second, when the sudden and catastrophic economic or political crisis hits, and the current concentrated political power fails, a new low reference point is naturally defined for the newcomers who will take over the political power. Once again, starting from such a low reference point, either the barely rational moves by the newcomers on duty, or the self-correction of external conditions, will result in significant positive developments in all economics, politics and international relations. And to make matters worse, the Social Intellect of the society will still be inadequate, as the previous concentrated political power has weakened it with utmost care. Therefore, it will not be difficult for the newcomers to over-accumulate the political support of the still naïve society immediately, and attain concentrated political power for themselves.

In short, *a sudden and catastrophic economic or political crisis may end the reign of the current concentrated political power, but only to replace it with another concentrated political power.* Therefore, *as long as the Social Intellect of the society remains to be inadequate, such crises may change the ruling concentrated political power but not the unfortunate fate of the society.* And again, the new concentrated political power will be equally motivated to keep the social awareness of the society as low as possible as long as possible, in order to sustain and strengthen its status as much as possible.

For that reason, it is in the best interest of the society not to tolerate any emergence of concentration of power in politics in the first place. However, that requires sustaining an adequate level of Social Intellect at all times, which, as explained before, is not possible in practise.

A Desperate Try To Prevent Concentration Of Power In Politics

From the very beginning of the establishment of the western social order based on Free Market Economy and Democracy, it was well known that what really matters for the stability and the well-functioning of this social order is the prevention of the concentration of power in politics.

Consequently, *to prevent the concentration of power in the political system and to secure the ultimate control of the society on political power, the concept of separation of powers within the political system is introduced in principle.* However, *whether its implementation in practise under the current democratic systems serves that principle well is another matter.*

The hidden primary assumption behind the principle is that, if separation of powers is achieved within politics, even though the Social Intellect of the society may weaken from time to time, and concentrations of power may emerge in the economy, the society will have enough time to recover its weakened Social Intellect to an adequate level without the risk of an emergence of concentrated political power in the meantime. And, as the political system continues to work well, once the Social Intellect of the society recovers, any concentrations of power in the economy that might have emerged can then be taken care of through the democratic system.

This principle of separation of powers within the political system is therefore the main insurance of the society against the concentration of political power and thus the sustainability of its social order. Unfortunately, although some structural separation of powers to prevent such concentration of political power seems to exist at the core of every democratic system, in practise the current structures are far from being adequate even in the democracies of the economically advanced western societies. The reasons and the cures for the failure of this vital principle will be discussed in Book Four of this series.

CONCLUSION

FAIR COMPETITION

Fair Competition, a concept beyond free competition, encompassing fair opportunity and the protection of the long-term interests of the society, must be the main pillar of Free Market Economy. And under Fair Competition, success in a competitive environment will primarily stem from merit, and not through luck, excessive risk taking or cheating.

The more a society approaches Fair Competition, the higher will be its economic growth rate and the lower will be the inequality within the society, and consequently, the higher will be the welfare of the society and the stronger will be the stability of its economic and political systems.

And therefore, the primary reason why a society should establish and guard Fair Competition, is not ethical values, but social wisdom.

ATTRACTION OF POWER & CHEATING

The trouble with power, both in economic and political senses, is that most competitors not only want to accumulate power, but to take it as far as possible and to keep it as long as possible. And even if power is initially attained through Fair Competition, in order to take it too far and to keep it for too long, eventually it will have to be used to eliminate Fair Competition, or actually any competition if possible. Then comes the natural urge for cheating.

CHEATING IS NOT A ZERO-SUM GAME

Cheating is not just an unfair transfer of benefits from one to another. As each Cheater extracts some benefit for himself, he simultaneously inflicts a much greater harm on the society, as he disrupts the optimal allocation of resources within the economy.

CHEATING FEEDS ON ITSELF

Once the Social Intellect of the society weakens and cheating starts, it feeds on itself and spreads in time, heavily harming the welfare of the whole society, including the Cheaters themselves - unfortunately beyond the recognition of all.

CHEATING AND CONCENTRATION OF POWERS

The spread of cheating in economics and politics eventually creates concentrated powers in both. And sooner or later these concentrated powers will start to cooperate with each other to further promote their interests against those of the society.

Cheating and the resulting concentration of powers eventually decrease economic growth way below its full potential and create excessive inequality, and consequently ruin both the welfare and the stability of the western social order.

POLITICS IS WHAT REALLY MATTERS

Even if cheating spreads and concentrated economic powers arise in the economy and in the markets, they can still be taken care of in time, as long as politics functions in the way it should. For that reason, the prevention of cheating and concentration of power in politics is a key condition for the well functioning and sustainability of the western social order.

THE AUTHOR

Salih Reisoglu has served as the CEO of an Investment Management Company for 20 years, and is an expert on Capital Markets with over 35 years of experience in analysing economics and politics. He is a regular guest speaker on many TV channels and universities. He holds an MSc in Computer Engineering from Lehigh University, and an MBA in Finance from The Wharton School of the University of Pennsylvania.

INDEX OF KEY CONCEPTS

ENDNOTES

[1] Welfare is not solely based on wealth, but also on the distribution of wealth within the society, i.e. inequality. The concept of welfare, and dynamics of change in welfare, will be discussed in detail in Book Three of this series.

[2] In the latest decades, the rise of globalisation resulted in the mutual integration of the economies of many societies, although the societies seem to be minimally aware of it. Moreover, the spread of electronic communication and the increase in labour mobility introduced a further dimension of integration in cultural aspects and thus inevitably in politics, while the societies are totally unaware of it. These developments caused a sudden and significant increase in the complexity of the world, and therefore a sudden and significant loss of Social Intellect in all societies, at a time when they were unprepared to deal with it. Today, the societies are strongly and immediately effected by almost any development at anywhere else in the world, totally out of their control, and they do not know how to handle such complexity.

[3] To visualise the complexity, consider a case where an output depends on three variables, namely x, y and z. In a linear relation, if you keep variables y and z constant, a unit change in variable x will cause a certain change on the output. But in a non-linear relation, even if you keep variables y and z constant, a unit change in variable x will cause a different amount of change on the output dependent on the current values of y and z. In practise, where there are too many non-linear variables and all are changing simultaneously, it becomes very difficult to understand and define the relation, and thus to forecast the output.

---

[4] "Misbehaving", Allen Lane (an imprint of Penguin Books), 2015, by Richard Thaler.

[5] The concept of Comparative Advantage was initially introduced by economist David Ricardo in the early 19th century, regarding the benefits of international trade and globalisation. But, the concept is also applicable to the analysis of the dynamics of economic growth, resource allocation and labour markets.

[6] Making rules but not enforcing them is the worst case scenario for the market: in case of lack of regulation, at least all the competitors remain on the same ground, however, when regulations exist but not enforced, they tie the hands of the Fair Players against the Cheaters, and as a consequence the Fair Players totally disappear and the society incurs the heaviest loss.

[7] In finance, not only the expected outcome, but also the variance of the potential outcomes (i.e. in very simple terms, the spread of the best and the worst potential outcomes, calculated based on statistical formulas) are taken into consideration. But regarding risk-taking capacity, it is not the variance but the magnitude of the potential most negative outcome that matters. Moreover, in finance, the final decision is based on risk-adjusted-returns, which simply means that, the magnitude of the return relative to the risk taken should be considered. In our simple illustration, project D is just a scaled up version of project C, so their returns with respect to the undertaken risks are similar.

[8] Although they are not common, there are cases where taking excessive risks are rational. One type of case that makes excessive risk taking rational is when a particular excessive risk may still be the best choice out of all the other available choices. Consider somebody with a terminal

illness with no known cure, who may take his chances -however slim they may be- with a newly developed treatment that is not well tested yet. When the low-risk path is a definite failure, taking an excessive risk may come out to be the rational choice. Another case that makes excessive risk taking rational is the behaviour of those who knowingly but willingly take excessive risks, including the extreme risk of sacrificing their own self, in order to protect the people or the principles they value. Consider the case of soldiers defending their country in a war.

[9] When actions based on negative expected outcomes are repeated for many times, as a natural rule of statistics, those sequences will always cumulate to give a net negative final result. Therefore, in the long run, those who take such risks will definitely fail and this will have nothing to do with bad luck. And since the repetition of such actions bring out the negative result, having enough risk taking capacity will be of no use.

[10] Every society with inadequate Social Intellect also has a media with inadequate intellect, which loves to present sexy stories of excessive-risk-taking, as these are effective attention attracters.

Rationality requires that a success story has to be a completed one that is tested and approved over time. As many excessive risk taking stories naturally end up in failure and misery in the long run, any media that sticks to this rule of rationality would refrain from advertising the wrong type of success stories and misguiding the society. Unfortunately, in most cases the media is not that patient, and presents cases of excessive risk taking to the society in mid-way while the risk takers are still travelling on borrowed fuel (like bank credit or venture capital) in their initial investment stages within a temporarily strong growth environment. Unfortunately, these cases are presented as if they are guaranteed to become sustainable success stories, although they will not in most cases. And most of the audience never learns what eventually happens at the very end, as the story will be long forgotten by the time it meets its destiny, which is much less sexy but much more miserable. Instead, the audience gets over-exposed to the very wrong idea that excessive risk taking is an admirable and desirable approach. And many members of the society, as principals or agents making strategic financing and investment decisions, just feel motivated, or even obliged, to take excessive risks.

And all gets worse when the economy gets red hot and the animal spirits take control of the decision making processes. Presentations of temporary success stories based on excessive risk taking while the economy is still hot, helps to speed up the spread of such risk taking behaviour to all the economy, worsening the overall outcome when the storm hits and a heavy price is paid by both the risk takers and the society.

[11] In practise, there is another component of the trouble: in many cases, the shareholders measure the success of their manager relative to the success of other managers, rather than relative to the risks taken. When such attitude is taken, the manager practically loses his freedom to manage the business rationally even if he wants to. A rational manager adjusts the risk taking decisions such that the company maximises its performance in the long-term, which requires some sacrifice of stellar performance in the short-term. However, when the evaluation is made relative to what the other managers have been doing in the short-term, the existence of a few irrationally excessive risk taking managers sets the benchmark for the rest of the managers. If the shareholders happen to expect an equivalent performance from their own manager in the short-term, the manager has no choice left but to mimic the excessive risk takers and take equally excessive risks to match their performance. Any manager who may fail to do so, is heavily punished by the shareholders as he is immediately diagnosed with under performance relative to their peers. But mimicking those excessive risks will ensure that their eventual destinies will be mimicked too. That is to say, when excessive risks are taken during the sunshine and then comes the rain, as it always does sooner or later, all those excessive risks will bring similar troubles that will massively hurt the performance of the company in the long-term, or even run it out of existence. Therefore, what initially looks like a trouble with the managers, as the agents, is actually a trouble with the

shareholders, as the principals, based on their misevaluation of the managers. Thus, if the shareholders want to prevent excessive risk taking, first they should give up taking other managers' performances as a benchmark, but rather focus on the rationality and the magnitude of the risks taken in their own company.

[12] When the bank lends to companies that all take calculated risks (case 1 in the illustration), the expected outcome for the bank is

Expected outcome for the *bank* (case 1) = 100%*(5%) = 5%

Thus, there is practically no case of failure. In case of success, the bank earns 5% on $10.000, thus $500. The depositors are paid 4% on their $9.000 deposit, taking away $360. The shareholders of the bank are left with $140, a return of 14% on their capital. Thus,

Exp. outcome for the *shareholders of the bank* (case 1) = 100%*(14%) = 14%

When the bank lends to companies that all take excessive risks (case 2 in the illustration), the expected outcome for the bank is

Exp. outcome for the *bank* (case 2) = 10%*(-100%) + 90%*(20%) = 8%

Thus, in case of failure, the shareholders of the bank lose $1.000 and the depositors lose $9.000. In case of success, the bank earns 20% on $10.000, thus $2.000. The depositors are paid 4% on their $9.000 deposit, taking away $360. The shareholders of the bank are left with $1640, a return of 64% on their capital. Thus,

Exp. outcome for the *shareholders of the bank* (case 2) = 10%*(-100%) + 90%*(64%) = 47.6%

[13] Being solvent practically means having adequate capital to absorb all potential credit losses that the bank may face. In our illustration, the bank that extends the risky credits becomes insolvent when the economy-wide crisis hits, as it loses all its capital and still can not absorb all the losses, thus defaults.

---

[14] When the expected outcome for the *shareholders of the banks* for case 2 are re-analysed, this time taking into account the negative effects of the economy-wide crises, and also assuming that while the banks are saved by the society all their capital will be lost, the situation remains to be a calculated risk taking behaviour for them, although with a lower long-term profitability. This is mainly because of the low frequency of economy-wide crises. To put simply, assume that, in the illustration, a shareholder of a bank invests $100 to the bank, and receives dividends of $48 for nine years (totalling $432), and then loses all his capital ($100) in a crisis at the tenth year. His overall wealth will end up to be $332. However, if the bank had only lended to low-risk companies (case 1) he would have accumulated 14% for 10 years on top of his capital, ending up at $240. Thus, in our illustration, in spite of a economy-wide crisis at the tenth year, the bank's lending to risk taking companies have benefitted the shareholder of the bank. Needless to say, in practise, on the one hand, the probabilities and outcomes may come out to be different than those in the illustration, reversing our conclusion. On the other hand, however, when the banks are saved by the society the capital of the shareholders are usually not erased completely, a fact supporting our conclusion.

[15] Please refer to "Economics for the Common Good", Princeton University Press, 2017, by Jean Tirole, pages 131-133.

[16] The increase in the total benefit of this little society of two people when the second -fairer- option is chosen, is not a mere design in the experiment, but actually a reflection of reality that we will explain in Section 4.4.

[17] As will be discussed in another book in the series, at the very heart of the trouble is the mishandling of globalisation. When coupled with the famous comparative advantage concept, which states that each producer has to focus on the product that it can produce better relative to others to

maximise overall efficiency and output, this creates a concentration of both economic interests and relevant information on a global scale. However, when each product, each one-out-of-a-zillion in the lives of the members of the global society, is supplied by an expert producer enjoying an extremely-concentrated benefit, and consumed by the whole global society, the concept of Concentrated Benefits vs Distributed Costs plays its strongest role and enables extreme-cheating.

[18] In mathematical terms, if $X = Y + Z$ (where X, Y, Z are all positive numbers), and if X is decreasing while Y is increasing, then the decrease in Z must be larger than the increase in Y. For example, if X decreases by 10 and Y increases by 2, Z must decrease by 12, as $(-10) = (+2) + (-12)$.

In our case, *Society = Cheater + Rest Of Society*

Thus, the decrease in X corresponds to the decrease in the overall wealth of the society, the increase in Y corresponds to the increase in the Cheater's wealth, and the decrease in Z corresponds to the decrease in the wealth of the rest of the society. It then follows that, the decrease in the wealth of the rest of the society has to be larger than the increase in the Cheater's wealth.

[19] Apart from the cases explained in this sub-section, there are also markets with a strategic significance for the security and/or the welfare of the society that should only be open to local competition, but not to global competition.

[20] For instance, refer to the article "Is big business really getting too big?" dated July 12th, 2023, at *The Economist*. A few sentences clarify the trend: "…That concentration has been rising is not in question. Across America's economy it is higher today than at any point in at least the past century. Out of some 900 sectors in America tracked by *The Economist*, the number where the four biggest firms have a market share above two-

thirds grew from 65 in 1997 to 97 by 2017. In Europe, where the data are less comprehensive, concentration has been increasing for at least 20 years. Using data on western Europe's largest economies—Britain, Germany, France, Italy and Spain—Gabor Koltay, Szabolcs Lorincz and Tommaso Valletti, three economists, find that the market share of the four largest firms grew in 73% of some 700-odd industries from 1998 to 2019. … The proportion of industries where the top four firms' share exceeded half increased from 16% to 27%. Britain and France saw the biggest jumps. …".

[21] For a simple illustration of the rising concentration of power and the emergence of monopolies in some markets, creating over-competition in others, consider the cases below. In each case, there are 5 markets and 100 competitors in the society.

<u>Case 1</u> : All markets are perfectly competitive and there is optimal allocation of resources in the economy.

Market	# Competitors	Status
A	22	optimal competition
B	18	optimal competition
C	21	optimal competition
D	19	optimal competition
E	20	optimal competition

	100	

<u>Case 2</u> : Concentration of economic power emerges in markets A, B, C, and free capital and thus competition starts to shift to the rest. Consequently, competition increases in markets D and E. Allocation of resources is distorted in the economy and starts to fall away from optimal.

Market	# Competitors	Status
A	12	decreased competition
B	11	decreased competition
C	13	decreased competition
D	29	increased competition
E	35	increased competition

	100	

Case 3 : Monopolies and oligopolies emerge and dominate markets A, B, C. Free capital flows further to the rest, increases competition further in markets D and E. A terrible misallocation of resources in the economy results. Practically market failures arise in all markets.

Market	# Competitors	Status
A	2	under-competition (oligopoly) / market failure
B	1	under-competition (monopoly) / market failure
C	3	under-competition (oligopoly) / market failure
D	46	over-competition / market failure
E	49	over-competition / market failure

	100	

[22] For instance, in the decades before the 2008 crisis, many Governments in the economically-developed western societies have chosen to under-regulate throughout the whole economy as a policy, and let too many concentrated economic powers or even monopolies emerge, which was one of the less-recognised structural reasons behind the crisis.

[23] As will be discussed in detail in Book Three of this series, welfare is not a direct function of wealth, but rather a combined outcome of wealth and inequality (i.e. the distribution of wealth) within a society. For that reason, welfare may actually be decreasing while wealth is increasing in case there is an excessive increase in inequality.